The Gaborro Reader 2

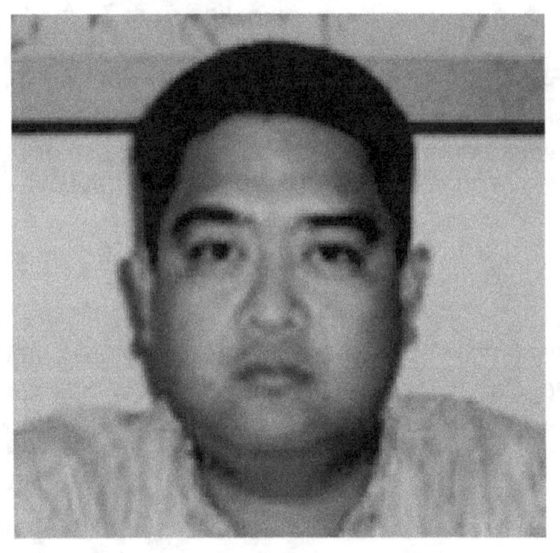

Allen Gaborro

Published by

TATAY JOBO ELIZES.
*Self-Publisher
in 2017, under the
permission and authorization*
of ALLEN GABORRO,
author and owner of the copyright to this book. The copyright owner can withdraw this permission at his discretion without any objection from Talay Jobo Elizes at any time. Printing of this book is using the present day method of Print-On-Demand (POD) system, where prints will never run out of copies to be available for posterity. The copyright owner is free to republish with other publishers anytime.

*ISBN - 13: 978 - 1977510280
ISBN - 10: 1977510280*

*Contact: job_elizes@yahoo.com
Website: http://tinyurl.com/mj76ccq*

Special Note

Articles are arranged at random dates

Contents

ooooo

About the Author

Allen Gaborro is a published author and an editor of young adult books. Published credits of Allen Gaborro include Private Character in the Public Eye. He continues to give me permission to use his latest articles and essays on numerous subject matter. I published his first book, The Gaborro Reader a few years ago.

This new book, The Gaborro Reader-2 is another compilation of his recent and current articles, that deserved to be archived in hard copy for posterity and availability to non-computer users. Also for future young gnerations.

Allen Gaborro is a resident book reviewer for the San Francisco-based Philippine News weekly. Allen has composed articles on historical, cultural, and political issues. Allen also has a bi-monthly column in the San Francisco-based FilAm Star newspaper. He is also working as a contributing international affairs writer for an English-language publication in Japan, as well as on a manuscript for a novel.

1

Andres Bautista: A Reflection of the Philippine Elite's Dysfunctionl Relationship with Society

Allen Gaborro
September 1, 2017

Allow me to preface this piece by stating that I am the first cousin of Patricia Bautista, the estranged wife of Philippine Commission on Elections (COMELEC) chief Andres Bautista. Although we are cousins, Patricia and I have not been in touch for several years now although this is not due to any acrimony between us. As fate would have it, we simply drifted apart over the years as can unfortunately happen to familial relations, particularly when they have resided half a world away from each other for most of their lives.

The fact that Patricia and I are related as first cousins could cause some to question the objectivity of what I have written below. Indeed, some could mistake me for being prejudiced by my blood connection to Patricia for I express views that I will admit, are sympathetic to her and critical of her husband. All I can say to that is, each reader will have to decide for themselves how much they are willing to take to heart and mind from what I have written. If readers cast doubt on my words because of my relation to Patricia Bautista then let that be their conclusion.

But I happen to believe that everything I have written here has suffered the wrath of my desire to always speak truth to power. The ideal reader should look for reason and logic in my comments and observations and not for glaring lapses of sentimentality for a beleaguered relation. For what it's worth, I am supporting Patricia's audacious—if arguably self-serving— move as something that is most certainly in the best interests of the Filipino nation.

***

I have to say that I'm not entirely surprised by the revelations of alleged corruption on the part of Comelec Chairman Andres Bautista. Rumors of his suspected financial malpractice— not to mention the hearsay on what has been described to me as his "compulsive" marital infidelities—have made the rounds over the past few years.

But merely discussing and spreading the rumors about Andres amounted to not much more than the dissemination of unsubstantiated *tsimis*. In other words, it was always intriguing to talk about the corruption and infidelity speculation, but there was never anything resembling hard evidence to prove either one. That is until now, what with the stunning discovery of suspicious financial documents by Andres's wife, Patricia (Tisha), in their conjugal home.

Upon hearing the jaw-dropping news, I communicated my support to Tisha by way of

Facebook. I told her that I was behind her one-hundred percent in coming forth in front of the media. In the presence of her interviewers, Tisha appeared composed and persuasive enough to convincingly raise the specter of her husband's financial malfeasance.

Conversely, I knew her skeptics would question Tisha's motives as they called to mind how tangled and contentious her marriage settlement negotiations with Andy had gotten. Some thought Tisha's gambit to be a maneuver to extract a fortune from Andy who claimed he had no such fortune. This is an oversimplification in light of everything that has happened.

Whatever her motives were, Tisha did the right thing. She put her well-being, and conceivably her physical safety, on the line by verbally highlighting glaring details of her husband's purportedly illicit activity. Tisha's decision goes to show that what I believe is Andy Bautista's arrogance, perhaps as much as the corruption allegations now besetting him, is what has him in hot water right now. It is a good bet that he never expected his outwardly soft-spoken and mild-mannered wife to rat him out. Ironically, Andy's smugness in regards to what he expected of his wife has made all the difference in upending and potentially destroying his professional life and his individual freedom.

One might surmise this arrogance stems from what could be an old-school Filipino attitude on the part of Andy, an attitude about marriage that bestows upon the husband the carte blanche to engage in any sort of sordid escapade he desires while the wife is consigned to the position of the silent, acquiescent bystander.

Having met and conversed with Andy a few times in the past, I was always struck by what I perceived to be his paradoxical disposition: he never failed to display an easy, down-to-earth temperament. But at the same time he evinced a subtle sense of conceit, an allusive air of superiority to anyone he was talking to. After taking these observations into account, we can deconstruct them and discover for ourselves how like a proverbial Machiavellian politician, Andy Bautista has worked his respectable public image so as to shroud the shadier reality behind it.

In a wider context, the Bautista scandal calls attention to the ongoing, dysfunctional relationship that the political and economic elites have had with the rest of Philippine society. Instead of unity and cooperation between the classes, the elite and their equally amoral, hypocritical lackeys—a deplorable list of sycophants and parasites that may include Andres Bautista—have devalued the legacy of national solidarity and consensus that was realized during EDSA I in 1986.

The lofty vision of the AmBisyon Natin 2040 public plan states that by 2040, "the Philippines shall be a prosperous, predominantly middle-class society where no one is poor." However, the way things are looking right now— especially under the murderous Duterte administration—that vision is more likely to be dashed as a result of the unremitting errors of judgment and failure of leadership on the part of the political and economic elite.

The legal predicament Andy Bautista finds himself in is just one of the latest illustrations of the top-heavy modern structure of corruption, cronyism, and criminality that has crowned Philippine politics and economy since the advent of American colonialism at the turn of the 20th century. Keeping that in mind, the dogged pursuit of justice in the case of Andres Bautista provides no guarantee that it will be served.

But for the millions of Filipinos who have experienced enough shame, guilt, and anger at the hands of the elite in almost complete anonymity, the process of bringing about lasting social justice, empowerment, and accountability in their country will get a huge lift by making sure that with Andres Bautista, any inexcusable misdeeds are dealt with firmly and fairly.

Ooooo

2

Duterte – Foe of Democracy
July 19, 2017

Philippine President Rodrigo Duterte is known for being one of those rare leaders who speak their mind without hesitation but more importantly, without regard to either domestic or international norms or sensitivities. This propensity towards blunt candor is pronounced when Duterte seethes against the entrenched structures of liberal democracy. Coming to power in what are unsettled political times around the globe, the last things that Duterte has expressed any sympathy for are the once-seemingly predestined universalism and absolutism of liberal democracy.

President Duterte has been an exemplar of the populist strongman narrative that has taken hold in several countries around the world including the Philippines. His approach to liberal democracy has been fused with nothing less than willful disdain and contempt. Fed up with liberal democracy's qualitative and quantitative flaws and failures in the Philippines, Duterte has treated democracy as no more than a regrettable experiment, some of the elements of which are being manipulated by him in the service of his creeping authoritarianism.

Duterte is following the standard of other anti-democratic figures and leaders such as Vladimir Putin, Donald Trump, Marine Le Pen, Abdel Fattah el-Sisi, and Recep Tayyip Erdoğan. No matter what they say in their public assurances to uphold the rule of law, these authoritarians if given enough opportunity, will strip democracy in their respective countries to the bone if they haven't already.

Why such widespread antipathy for democracy? Some 25 years ago, it was easy for one to have thought that liberal democracy was the premium socio-political and economic path left to mankind after the collapse of communism at the end of the Cold War. Political scientist Francis Fukuyama triumphantly told us so back then what with his judgment that we had reached the figurative "End of History."

But Fukuyama's End of History, while ushering in an era of tremendous benefits for millions around the planet, would also drag a comparable number over the precipice of deprivation and disillusionment. Liberal democracy and post-Cold War capitalism have proven to be what Plato might have called a "pharmakon": something that is both a cure and a poison at the same time. While the liberal democratic and capitalist ethos has brought democracy and prosperity to so many who previously could never have dreamed of such ideals coming to fruition, it failed to take into account the swathes of populations that would be left behind socially, economically, and politically.

The presidency of Rodrigo Duterte is a political product of that monumental failure as its scope expanded in the Philippines. Duterte emerged as a viable presidential candidate amidst the interminable despoiling of the Philippine economy and political system. The 1986 EDSA phenomenon was supposed to put an end to rampant economic corruption and fundamental abuse of the political system, as well as pull lower class Filipinos out of poverty and give them a chance for a better future.

But the lofty promise of EDSA 1986 was outrun by the hard and grievous realities on the ground. For one thing, self-proclaimed defenders of freedom and equality among the Philippine elite showed their true colors by working to preserve and strengthen their economic and political monopoly throughout the whole post-EDSA 1986 process leading up to Duterte's election.

As a result, whatever advantages that emerged out of the popular revolt were tilted heavily towards the elite. Inevitably, the Filipino masses would find it hard to believe the EDSA reformers whenever the pledges of February 1986 were invoked. In reflecting the disenchantment of the masses, Duterte stated that EDSA did restore democracy but that today, more than a quarter century after the fact, "the economic and social structure remains a lopsided equation in favor of the few and the many are poor and neglected."

Therefore those among the intelligentsia and educated segments of Philippine society should not have been astonished by Duterte's rise to the pinnacle of Philippine politics. Open to the influence of a big-talking, expletive-laden, recalcitrant autocrat whose political career has been defined by blood and murder, millions of Filipinos have formulated some general socio-political truths about their lives, truths about how their Job-like patience in their leaders has gone for naught. Or truths that say the game of life in the Philippines is perpetually rigged against them, the needy and underprivileged of society. Or truths that conclude that their political leaders never have and never will come clean for them.

In looking through the magnifying glass, it's easier to see how that simply asserting that many ignorant and uneducated Filipinos voted Rodrigo Duterte into the presidency does not get to the deeper issues surrounding the foundation of his ascendancy. The magnifying glass tells us that it was ultimately the mistakes, the neglect, and the exploitation on the part of the Philippine elite that spawned the vain and sadistic overlord Filipinos see at the helm before them. Now it is too late: all Filipinos will have to reap the real world consequences of his anti-democratic and dictatorial message and actions.

ooooo

3

The Fraud and Folly of Duterte's Drug War

Dateline, Feb. 28, 2017

President Rodrigo Duterte's extrajudicial killings (EJK) of drug dealers and addicts are becoming an emotionally-charged undertaking but not necessarily for the reasons many think. Supporters of Duterte's explicitly violent anti-drug campaign focus on how savagely effective it has been in ostensibly emancipating Philippine society from the scourge of the illegal drug industry. It must be a highly emotional thing for Filipinos to think that they have finally begun retiring drug crime to the ash heap of history.

Except that this conclusion is as fallacious as it is contemptible. But I will get back to the contemptible aspect of it later. I first want to tackle the notion that the EJK killings—which are tantamount to "act(s) of terrorism" according to James Fenton of the New York Review of Books—are in no small part an emotionally-charged phenomena, a phenomena that is running both political cover and interference for

Rodrigo Duterte as he boastfully plays the role of the merciless, take-no-prisoners president.

It's not hard to see why so many Filipinos have turned a blind eye towards the cruelty and illegality of the drug killings. On the surface, the killings appear to have dealt a severe blow to the illegal drug industry. Duterte supporters point to the growing absence of drug dealers and users on the streets. Those same dealers and users used to be able to conduct their illicit business and behavior on the streets with impunity. The Duterte faithful have presumed that—on the basis of that observable absence along with the all too familiar scenes of dead bodies sprawled out for all to see—that the drug dealers and users have been permanently dissuaded from practicing their dark trade and from feeding their addictions.

Nothing could be farther from reality. The absence can be explained by the likelihood that the drug dealers and users have simply gone underground. More and more, dealers and users are avoiding the murderous police forces and vigilantes by going behind closed doors and engaging in other forms of concealment, thereby becoming invisible to the extent where people think they have been put out of commission for good. This is the bogus line that Duterte is trying to push onto Filipinos. It is folly to believe that the killings, as pitiless as they are, have persuaded drug pushers and users to suddenly stop on a dime what they have been doing for so long. It goes without saying that just because you cannot see something doesn't mean that it doesn't exist. Like with terrorism, you cannot eradicate or even diminish the drug trade solely by the barrel of a gun no matter how high you ratchet up the body count.

Drug usage and distribution are symptoms not causes. While not the lone cause, extreme poverty has long been associated with the prevalence of drugs in a society and for good reason. Anyone living an impoverished existence as millions of Filipinos do will desperately seek some kind of escape, however temporary, from that harsh reality. Drugs provide such an escape for those unfortunate souls. The undeniable fact that Duterte has concentrated his drug war primarily on the easiest targets—the lower classes—only adds salt to the wound.

This is not to justify drug trafficking or consumption in any way. But Duterte's unwillingness to comprehend and address the roots of drug crime and abuse—and instead pursue a disproportionate, short-sighted policy that principally targets the manifestations of the drug trade rather than its cardinal underpinnings—is the product of a grievously unaccountable, undemocratic, and distressingly facile strategy. Its repercussions lead to greater human suffering, something the Philippines doesn't need any more of.

Right up to the latest drop of blood spilled as a result of his pigheaded crusade, it is in Rodrigo Duterte's political interests to keep the spotlight on his war against the drug trade. That is why I wrote above that there is something contemptible about Duterte's anti-drug campaign other than the carnage that it has generated. That there is something contemptible with Duterte's campaign shouldn't be so surprising as murder and politics have intersected each other more than once in his controversial past.

For one thing, the president is far too clever not to know that sending drug dealers and users to meet their maker is not a deterrent. For Duterte, the drug killings are the means to a more expedient end. He is using his drug war as a cover for his private lack of confidence about being able to implement far-reaching socio-economic reform, long overdue reform that would necessitate major poverty alleviation programs for the benefit of the lower classes.

Why would Duterte be uneasy about effectuating fundamental anti-poverty initiatives, "fundamental" being the key word here? Drastically improving the lives of the masses was after all, a primary theme of his presidential campaign. He is reluctant because he perceives that anti-poverty initiatives—initiatives that should begin to take on the Philippines' socio-economic structural deficiencies—will be too difficult to engender in a top-heavy, highly stratified society in which an elite class essentially monopolizes the country's financial and natural resources. The entrenched Philippine elite would certainly oppose any progressive reform initiatives as a threat to their historic dominance.

In making a cold political calculation, Duterte has determined that the bringing about of game changing anti-poverty initiatives is not worth the large expenditures of time, energy, and political capital that would be required to counterbalance the economic and political elite. Based on his actions or lack thereof, to say that Duterte's bark is worse than his bite when it comes to the entrenched elite is no exaggeration.

Accordingly, Duterte needs his illegitimate drug war to conceal his political cowardice in doing what is best in the long run for the Filipino people. Duterte is utilizing a tried-and-tested strategy of mass distraction for as long as he can get away with it. The tragedy of it all is that according to Amnesty International, more than a thousand people are being killed every month under the aegis of Rodrigo Duterte's homicidal anti-drug push. Overall, some 7,000 have been dispatched since its inception, the vast majority of them having been denied due process of law.

There's no use running away from these disturbing numbers. They lie at the heart of Rodrigo Duterte's hellish version of peace and order and his Machiavellian leadership. It remains unknown how long the Philippines can continue on this treacherous path. That is to say, when will the powerless stop paying for the sins and ambitions of Rodrigo Duterte?

Ooooo

4

Rodrigo Duterte: Back to the Future

Dateline: November 14, 2016

A common thread that I am finding in the responses to my criticisms of Philippine president

Rodrigo Duterte is that I should give the man a chance before I drive hard against his words and actions. Respondents have suggested instead that I reallocate my energies for a much later time when we would be better able to assess and evaluate Duterte's performance.

The reasoning that has been put forth by these respondents as they take issue with my criticism of the Philippine president converges on a frame of reference which is centered around the overdue need for reform. However, the way the respondents have defended that frame of reference is incompatible with one of the important lessons of analyzing political leaders: ignore the past at your peril for it is ever-present in the ways and means of how rulers will exercise power.

The last thing Duterte supporters want to hear is that the most vociferous in their praise of him run the risk of becoming the most vociferous in their disapproval of the president down the road. As they applaud him for his ruthlessly violent stance against drug-related crime—as if in and of itself killing suspected drug users and dealers alone will stop drug crime in the country—Duterte supporters constantly remind us that "change" is what it's all about and that only he can carry out that change as a leader who is tough and strong and who will do what is in the best interests of the Filipino people.

But what the Duterte supporters ignore is the historical truism that how someone comes to power will be exactly the way they will rule once in power. To put it differently, the past is a valuable resource in prognosticating the future with Duterte at the helm of the country.

Duterte's political past raises many eyebrows for his alleged involvement in the so-called Davao death squads which are believed to have extra-judicially taken the lives of hundreds of people in the city for crimes, real and imagined. Duterte has freely and without remorse admitted his complicity in the killings and has even bragged about their bloody effectiveness in reducing crime in Davao.

But in using excessive lethal force without due process of law undermines the very notion of law and order that forms Duterte's political center of gravity. To circumvent the rule of law in order to enforce law and order is an example of the narrow sophistry and rationalizing that is a trademark of President Duterte's governing style. Maintaining law and order by breaking it is the height of hypocrisy and the absence of common sense and reason. Duterte however, has parlayed this into a winning narrative among his voters.

There is something to be said for the overall conclusion that Duterte has reached on the U.S.-Philippine relationship. Since its genesis in the turn-of-the-century American colonization of the archipelago, it has been a hegemonic patron-client relationship to be sure and on that account Filipino nationalists have said that Duterte is justified in reliving the painful memories of how it has—materially, physically, culturally, and psychologically—highlighted American strength and at the same time underscored Philippine weakness and dependency.

A singular take-home for Duterte from the history of the US-Philippine relationship is his near-scathing indignation at a specific episode in America's historically-checkered role in the islands. It involved a 2002 explosion in the Davao hotel room of Michael Terrence Meiring, a US citizen who had been indicted for possessing explosives. Before any case could be pursued, Meiring mysteriously disappeared. Davao mayor Duterte believed that the US government had somehow wielded its magical wand of neo-colonial machinations in enabling Meiring to escape justice. Duterte has understandably never forgotten that incident. Indeed, what has become a ritual response for Duterte in his critical scrutiny of America's constructive yet controversial history in the Philippines has been laced with defiance and bitterness and filled with invective towards the former colonizer and long-time patron.

A far more distant historical event that Duterte talks about with rancor is the massacre of 600 Moros at the hands of American soldiers in 1906. Hardly one to expound upon the necessity of forgiveness when acting as the protagonist, Duterte has demanded an apology from the United States for the massacre which took place on Jolo Island in the southernmost reaches of the Philippine island chain. What became known as the Bud Dajo massacre occurred against the backdrop of America's counterinsurgency operations against Moro rebels who resisted the colonial occupation of their land.

Duterte has tried to sear these two historical moments—along with his general enmity towards the United States—into the contemporary Filipino consciousness to the same pathological extent he has carved it into his own. And yet, Duterte does so with great irony. About the president and his insights on the United States, novelist Gina Apostol writes: "An abuser condemned an earlier abuser of the nation in order to sanction his own abuse."

Duterte has been able to project his antipathy towards the US government's neo-colonial policies into a national policy of his own. It is a policy that is slowly turning US-Philippine relations on their head. It is also a policy loaded with a range of unintended consequences not the least of which is the appeasement of a repressive dictatorship in China. China, with its exertive ambitions on maritime territories in the South China Sea—some of which are legally under Philippine sovereignty—potentially represents a clear and present danger to the Philippines.

One only has to open their eyes to Duterte's political past as a brutally honest, uncompromising mayor and presidential aspirant to see how it informs his thought processes as president. The atrocious acts of guilty-until-proven-innocent violence perpetrated against thousands of suspected drug dealers and users and his precipitous disruption of vital US-Philippine ties both arise out of the recesses of his public past.

The problem with the Duterte defenders that I have heard from is that they disregard what his past has to say about how he would conduct himself as president. It was Duterte after all, who as a mayor and presidential candidate advocated extrajudicial killings—irrespective of any human collateral damage—to fight the drug trade. It was mayor Duterte who shouted from the mountaintop his aversion towards America and who as presidential candidate telegraphed that he was willing to jeopardize relations with the United States—an impeachable but indispensable ally nevertheless—for both historical and personal affronts. It was candidate Duterte who threatened to abolish the Philippine Congress if its members did not facilitate the passage of his policies. And it was first as mayor and then as presidential candidate that Duterte unconscionably called for the burial of former dictator Ferdinand Marcos as an undeserved national hero.

Nothing that Duterte says and does consequentially as president, now and in the future, cannot be traced back to the record of his dubious, pseudo-democratic public past, a past that has been glossed over with his populist, anti-establishment, everyman image by his hordes of disaffected supporters.

The respondents' sentiment that at any rate—his contentious past notwithstanding—Duterte is an agent of change so therefore he's better than no change at all is the definition of self-deception. Change has to be implemented responsibly, compassionately, and sensibly. To implement it thoughtlessly and full speed ahead simply for the sake of change itself is going too far, too fast. In other words, the cure should not be worse than the disease. Change is only a salutary preoccupation if it is sown with unmistakable empathy and judiciously maximized to such a fundamental level as to be truly meaningful.

When the regrets start pouring in over the course of time with Rodrigo Duterte, it will be too late. The damage will have been done. Then Filipinos will hit themselves over the head as they ask themselves, as they did with Marcos, Estrada, and Macapagal-Arroyo, and with countless other politicians, why they enabled these individuals, individuals they knew in their hearts to have questionable ethics and morals, to rise to the pinnacle of power.

ooooo

5

Rodrigo Duterte: More Illusion Than Fact
Dateline: March 5, 2016

The main choices in the 2016 Philippine presidential election are clear cut. They are either more-of-the-same, entrenched political establishment types or they are the new, fresh starters on the presidential aspirant block who indignantly arch their brows at traditional politics and politicians, but naively or craftily promise the moon to disillusioned voters from an ivory tower

Davao City mayor Rodrigo Duterte is one such contender for the top national office. As a provocateur and contrarian, he illustrates the collision between traditional politics and the populist, anti-establishment political

narrative. However, Duterte's opposing vision has offered little beyond the most cursory and reductionist assumptions and prescriptions for the country.

Throughout modern political history, individuals aiming for national office have spoken reverently of their collective themes and platforms. In his capacity as a candidate, Duterte has spoken reverently of his own views but in such a style and tone that it reflects his conviction that he is subject to no one outside of himself. Duterte has brought forth his understanding of the pressing issues that beset the Philippines with all the vanity and self-certitude he can muster.

Duterte's braggadocio about what he would do as president has shown that he has taken little time to delve deeply into the major issues confronting the Philippines. For example, he has treated the democracy vs. discipline debate as an easily resolved dilemma. Having no better testimony than his uncompromising corpus of work as Davao mayor, Duterte has suggested that he would slow the democratic process down because of the chaos and disorder he believes it leads to. Indeed, he has stated that he is ready and willing to abolish the Philippine congress if his proposed reforms are not passed.

Duterte's political mind is shared with authoritarians the world over: turmoil generally arises from giving people too much freedom so the authoritarian thinking goes. Over the centuries, every authoritarian worth his or her salt has intrinsically ascribed to this notion. As a subscriber to this view, Duterte has the perfect makings of a dictator in the wings. He will brook little dissent from any corner once in power.

Filipino voters seek a leader who can apprehend their fears, feelings, needs, and expectations as they have grown weary of a political establishment that pays lip service to their right to live and prosper as decent human beings. The 2016 election is going to mean everything to Filipinos as they look for a candidate from an alternate socio-political universe rather than from the old school what with its solid array of craven, duplicitous, and ineffectual leaders.

But Filipino voters should be careful of what they wish for they are as mentally and emotionally vulnerable as they have ever been in a presidential election season. Instead of deliberating with their minds, too many Filipinos are impulsively listening to their hearts as they search for the leader that has the tidiest prescriptions for the most complicated of the nation's problems. Politicking on the tailwind of a populist wave, Rodrigo Duterte appeals to this susceptible mass audience as he leads it on a crusade to bring law and order to the nation.

As his campaign gathers speed, Duterte's aptitude for making quixotic pledges becomes all too plain to see and hear. He tells Filipinos that he would utilize both the armed forces and the police to "wipe out" (i.e. kill) all criminals as if that could be accomplished without violating any human rights. Cleaning up crime and corruption is always commendable. But if there is any truth to the accusations of human rights violations during his stint as Davao mayor, it would portend a path towards authoritarian rule for Duterte if he were to become president.

Duterte has gone on to blithely promise that he will end traffic in the overcrowded Metro Manila area, eliminate corruption in just a few months time, and make vague statements about improving the economy. Far from being realistic, Duterte's promises are more significant for their lack of concreteness than for their viability. Duterte comparisons have been made with another smug, narcissistic, and boastful nonconformist presidential candidate in the United States, Donald Trump. For both, the devil is truly in the details as they avoid revealing any in their promises.

Opportunistic politicians like Rodrigo Duterte and Jejomar Binay are commanding voters' attention by clarifying, rationalizing, and reprising their themes and positions with strong doses of sophistry and misdirection. It is what these conniving politicians do best----blow smoke up their constituents' asses and pull excrement out of their own.

Rodrigo Duterte, both as a public servant and as a presidential candidate, is more illusion than fact. No more is this obvious than in the misguided sentiment he has generated among his staunchest supporters. To them, Duterte is the hailed individual, the familiar male protagonist who has found the sweet spots in their socio-political consciousness and left a delusionary trail of gold for them to follow.

In voting for a new president, Filipinos should pursue their passion for change but temper it with common sense and the dictates of reason. What should count as a wise decision for president is an individual possessing the steady disposition, perspicacity, inner strength, compassion, and patience required of any democratic leader. Taking a frantic leap of faith with a candidate like Duterte does away with all those virtues and instead invites further enmity, inequality, marginalization, and oppression.

Ooooo

6.

Terrorism and Its Capitalist Discontents
Dateline, August 16, 2016

The Islamic State (IS) imagines that anyone and everyone is old enough to die. As a member of IS, that deadly prerequisite comes with the territory---the lives of men, women, and children however innocent, are redefined as necessary casualties in the war against the infidels. But the Islamic State's dissonance with the values of Western liberal humanism not only arises out of the violently messianic ideological commitment of its members to a radical interpretation of Islam, it also spews from a depth and scale of hatred so intense that it is barely comprehensible to the rational mind.

For an IS member to cold bloodedly murder their fellow human beings all in the name of a "holy" cause does indeed take a lot of hatred and intolerance. But what is the deeper cause of that hatred and intolerance? Or to put it more precisely, what makes someone amenable to a sentiment so venomous and fatal? I believe that the cause is centered more around external pressures than it is around religion.

There are competing theories as to why IS will stop at nothing to harm others on both a local and mass scale. Can we chalk it up to the Freudian idea of the primeval cruelty embedded within human nature? Or is it something more exterior to human nature, something more socially and historically structural, especially when we are talking about living in the materialistic, consumptionist cage fight that is a modern capitalist society?

Anyone who has ever lived in a modern capitalist society doesn't have to be told that it has its risks and pitfalls. When the pain of those risks and pitfalls are felt so acutely there arises the distinct possibility that the afflicted will begin to trace within themselves the outlines of a deprived and alienated inner self. As those feelings come together and coalesce into a hardened core, it produces a traumatized self. And as any traumatized self is wont to do, it desperately seeks the order and certainty and meaning that it struggles to find in modern existence. If it cannot find what it's looking for in the everyday mainstream, the traumatized self can fall prey to dangerous ideologies and attitudes like those espoused by the Islamic State which offers it much of what a modern capitalist life can fail so miserably to do.

The internal psychological conflicts that all humans undergo are evidently clear in a winner-take-all capitalist existence. These conflicts are over any number of issues: love, race, religion, sex, money, power, etc. The easiest way to deal with them is for some to lash out, to blame someone else for their misfortune. Tragic outcomes aside, it's quite understandable if the affected individual is bent and broken mentally and emotionally and scarred perhaps for life. This is the dark side of the modern capitalist system that many find impossible to ignore. Its institutionalized costs can bring out the worst in people and compel them into "losing it" as we say and advance to the stage of taking measure for measure in regards to their perceived mistreatment.

There is a limitation to this externally systemic gravitation. No human being is born with a blank slate of a consciousness. Every person is born with some pre-birth level of innate knowledge. Their self-identities and ways of seeing the world are partially constructed and governed by that pre-existential knowledge. But this does not appreciably mitigate the role that the thicket of external contingencies play in the evolution of an individual's character. Karl Marx was largely on the right track when he wrote, "It is not the consciousness of men that determines their being, but, on the contrary, their social being that determines their consciousness."

Against the tide of those who oversimplify by chastening the distressed of a capitalist society to look at no one else but themselves in the mirror, what has happened in San Bernardino, Orlando, Istanbul, Dhaka, Nice, and Munich, and in other cities around the globe did not originate somewhere in the deep recesses of the perpetrators' souls. Rather than having an organic basis, these vile acts are more likely the result of a highly-predatory, exclusionary socio-economic system that estranges the multitudes who cannot cope with its unreasonable demands. It is an elitist, dysfunctional, and schizophrenic form of capitalism that subordinates ethics and morality to the sidelines and exerts its take-no-prisoner philosophy relentlessly and ruthlessly.

We are all beholden to the structural, environmental, and civilizational stimuli inherent in a modern society. No one is immune to the price that has to be paid to conform to it. This underscores the societal challenge that lays in front of those who are least able to cope with it. All the military action, all the counterintelligence, and all the universal goodwill and humanism will not be enough to defeat IS without a fuller understanding of the societal interplay of capitalist drives, dictates, and desires that can turn the most anodyne of people into monsters.

ooooo

7
President Duterte, But For How Long?

Dateline, June 10, 2016

If there is any credence to vice-presidential loser Bongbong Marcos's claim that there is a covert plan to remove president-elect Rodrigo Duterte from office by way of impeachment within the early stages of his administration, it will send a strong message that at the cusp of historic national development—a development comparatively on par with other emerging economies around the globe—that the Philippines is flirting with a moral threshold, a threshold that has gradually taken shape since the country broke free of dictatorial rule thirty years ago.

The threshold I speak of lies between having the unmistakable chance of a peaceful and prosperous future and exorcising the interminable ghost of an underachieving, degraded past. Having entrusted the presidency to Rodrigo Duterte, a solid plurality of Filipino voters are attempting to put the past in its place and go all out on a limb for real change. Duterte for them, represents the cure for the once seemingly-incurable malady that is a rigged, monopolistic, and kleptocratic socio-economic and political system.

To his supporters, Duterte is a transformational force imbued with an overarching spirit of vigor and of being what in the

Philippines would traditionally be considered a "real man": a semi-alpha male who talks tough and forthrightly in the perfect freedom of an unfettered vernacular, and who is not afraid to take decisive action. This translates into Duterte's effective ability to connect with the Filipino voter. In turn it has made it easy for people to identify with "Digong".

Many common readings of Duterte's election have suggested that if we were to follow the trail of his victory, we would see that it leads to the psychological breaking point of the low information, deficiently-educated, disillusioned Filipino who understandably has had enough of unprincipled elitist politics. Now, as a clear-cut alternative, Duterte has been chosen to relieve Filipinos' capacity for division and hardship at the hands of a self-referential elite.

But the story of Rodrigo Duterte's election entails more than a rich/poor, common folk/elite dichotomy. Basking in the respect and admiration of his supporters, Duterte has spun a narrative that he comes from a modest and unassuming background. As compelling as that narrative appears to be to many, the deeper truth of the matter is that Duterte hails from a family that has made its historical mark as a political dynasty in the southern Philippines. In other words, the president-elect's talk about being a natural foil of the political elite comes with a qualification, one that beset Corazon Aquino and her administration's efforts to deal with agrarian reform. Can Duterte take the lead in cleaning up the excesses of the elite when his family background exudes elitism?

Skeptics questioned Corazon Aquino's ability to implement bold agrarian reform during her tenure. She was after all, a member of the same privileged landowning class whose properties her government was ostensibly out to reform. Duterte likewise is, behind his unpretentious, down-to-earth exterior, a proud lion of an elite legacy. As the streetwise, *enfant terrible* of Philippine politics, Duterte has never forgotten his family's privileged political heritage even as he has taken stinging potshots at the country's ruling elite. He has gone so far as to assert that the elite are a "threat to democracy."

So how are we to reconcile Duterte's political lineage with his contentious comments on the elite? To put it in some perspective, Duterte has expressed a vision for the Philippines that is potentially at odds with the local hegemons and power brokers that fill out the upper rungs of political and economic life. He has proposed major changes ranging from some form of meaningful wealth redistribution to resolutely eliminating corruption at the highest levels of society and government. Duterte has also sent a loud and clear message that he would terminate the Philippine Congress—an institution rife with elitists—if they do not pass his legislative agenda. At what point will the ruling elite give in to their darkest instincts and defend by all means necessary their core interests against Duterte's advances? Are Duterte and his detractors among the elite on a collision course? Are there elitist elements who are conspiring to dramatically unseat a President Duterte if they believe that things aren't going their way?

Which all leads us back to Bongbong Marcos's heads-up of a planned overthrow of Duterte. Although we should take Marcos's warning with a serious grain of salt—the son of the former dictator is hardly the last word, or the first for that matter, on the veracity of such intrigue—even so Filipinos seem serenely unaware that such a drastic scenario as a government takeover could take place and thereby reverse the results of the 2016 presidential election.

However, a scenario that would force Duterte into abandoning his electoral victory is not beyond the realm of possibility. For some, such a move defies logic for it would mean the overt subversion of democracy in the Philippines. When Egyptian President Mohamed Morsi was removed from office in an extra-constitutional action in 2013, one of the primary excuses—an excuse condoned by many Egyptians as well as by the West—for his being unseated was that Morsi was allegedly paving the way for Islamic sharia rule. An extra-constitutional change of government in the Philippines lacking a similarly convincing pretext would earn the punitive ire of the international community and cause a frontal breach in the already-strained relationship between democracy and order, as well as between the powerful and the governed in the country.

Filipinos like to pride themselves on their cultural heritage, on their general sense of optimism, and on their ubiquitous bonhomie and geniality. But they also pride themselves on their post-authoritarian democratic ethos and system of government, notwithstanding its ethical perversions and moral compromises and repertoire of financial scandals and popular uprisings. Ever since the demise of the Marcos dictatorship, Filipinos have drawn a line in the sand when it comes to protecting their democracy whenever it has come under duress. They are not about to be indifferent if either the Philippine elite or Rodrigo Duterte or other actors in positions of power and authority attempt to rein it in for their self-serving motives.

ooooo

8

Image is the Reality:
Trump and Duterte
Dateline, May 5, 2016

Imagine being chained in a chair in a cave. You are chained along with a host of other individuals in such a way that all of you can only see straight ahead without being able to turn sideways in either direction and without being able to glance backwards. What is visible to you is a large screen in front of you and the shadows that are moving across it. Imagine that you and the rest of the captive audience that you are a part of have known nothing other than the shadows; you can be forgiven for believing that they are reality.

But then there is a revealing moment, a moment in which you break loose of your chains. At that moment, your consciousness begins to open to the possibility that there is a more bonafide reality hidden behind the screen "reality" of shadows. However, the problem is no longer simply to seek the reality that lies beyond the screen, but to convince your still chained compatriots that what they have been seeing on the screen since they can remember is nothing but superficial images and errant illusions. Despite your best efforts you not only fail to persuade the rest of the audience of the deception that has been perpetrated on them, but you get them so indignant at you for trying to burst their delusions that they reject you as an interloper. Some would say that you are better off getting back in your seat and keeping your mouth shut.

What I am alluding to here is Plato's famous allegory "Parable of the Cave." The metaphorical tale is relevant to the public discourse and debate that Filipino voters in the Philippines and American voters in the United States have had to contemplate in their respective countries' 2016 presidential election campaigns.

Whoever came up with the idea that "image is everything" or that "perception is everything" wasn't kidding. Nowhere is this more true in politics, particularly when it comes to campaigning. More particularly when it comes to campaigning for the highest office in the land, the presidency. It's been no secret that over the years, presidential candidates in both the

Philippines and the United States have become reliant on the professional manufacturing and packaging of their public images. And why not? Reaping the harvest of their meticulous image-making has brought untold benefits and advantages for political clienteles the world over.

I suppose that at its essence there is nothing wrong with the utilitarian contriving of images except when it is used to deliberately deceive electorates. Let's be honest: it is a rare thing for voters to see through all the smoke and mirrors of the political imagery that is peddled to them. Indeed, rarely do voters *want* to see the reality behind all the imagery. Like the chained prisoners in Plato's cave, far too many voters allow themselves to be fooled into believing a comforting illusion rather than uncover the hard truth hidden behind it.

Considering that the majority of Filipinos are living in socioeconomic destitution and have been so for a very long time, it would almost be a pity to disparage their need for comforting illusions. They don't see the images put before them as such. Out of these conjured images come self-styled heroes or champions that anyone in any kind of distress can relate to and believe in and follow until the ends of the earth. Until very recently, such compelling and vigorous political saviors were hard to come by in the Philippines and in the United States. Now both countries have simultaneously spawned two false prophets for disillusioned voters to follow on the primrose path.

Donald Trump in the US and Rodrigo Duterte in the Philippines have rocked the political establishment mold and reworked it to make it look foreign to the political generations that came before them. Both men's indulgent and provocative rhetoric and propaganda are their ways of evening the score with the ossified establishment, of leveling out the political playing field for the discontented, the disenfranchised and otherwise marginalized.

Guided by the spirit of a resurgent populism, Trump and Duterte are the surging princelings of a new political composition, a composition that is intended to shatter the junction of elitist politics and the corruptive influences of money. The aggregate of causes of what has become fractious, unpopular, and dysfunctional governments on both sides of the Pacific are all on record. Therefore, in asking ourselves what business does two loutish and monosyllabic blowhards like Trump and Duterte have in offering themselves as legitimate presidential candidates, we must decisively call into question the commitment that American and Filipino political leaders profess for the well-being of their constituents. Knowing what we know about how politics is done in Manila and Washington today, I think it's safe but regrettable to say that there is reasonable cause for the Dutertes and Trumps of the world to emerge out of their holes to spout their venom and vulgarities for every feeble-minded, easy prey voter within reach.

However, when confronted with tough questions about planning and policy in detail, Trump and Duterte run for cover behind their public images which are tight-knit safe havens for them to hide behind when any kind of adversity strikes. They go on as before, having voters take them on presentation and trust even as both men avoid direct answerability and accountability for their past and present actions and statements. Trump and Duterte get away with it because their cunningly-crafted images are effective political tools in a period that is ripe for the ascendancy of anti-establishment, insurgent candidates in the US and in the Philippines.

Political imagery has long been a fixture of modern politics. It has been one of politicians' greatest instruments as they traverse trials and tribulations on the long, difficult road to the presidency. But everything in politics is relative: what might be appealing, empathetic, galvanizing illusions—even if they are overreaching—will always be preferable to a solid and penetrating truth for many Filipino and American voters. That is the power of the image. That is the power of Donald Trump and Rodrigo Duterte.

ooooo

9.
Educating the Filipino Voter

Dateline, March 26, 2016

In my last article, I had written about Philippine presidential candidate Rodrigo Duterte and his steady procession of ill-defined promises, controversial comments and attitudes, and delusionally proposed courses of action.

I have received several responses to that article which have made me appreciative of their authors' feelings. Generally speaking, the respondents felt that my article fell short of getting the message across to Rodrigo Duterte's most receptive audience, the denizens of the discontented masses. The focal point of my message was that Duterte was snookering his vulnerable followers into believing that the toughest problems besetting the Philippines could be solved firstly by distilling them down to the most simplistic terms, and then by outlining those problems in such a way that they appear as if they could be decisively resolved with little more than the assertion of firm, resolute leadership.

The respondents reminded me that many of Duterte's supporters tend to be commonplace, low information citizens who have not been fortunate enough to have had a proper formal education. The bulk of Duterte's supporters, like the man himself, are unmoored from the reality of what is possible and are instead clinging blindly to his sometimes deliberate, sometimes impetuous equivocations. Therefore, how could one provoke objective argument and discussion about Duterte's (or Jejomar Binay's for that matter) candidacy among his supporters and make them see the light?

The best answer I can come up with is to place the onus on the educated Filipino middle and intellectual classes. They must do whatever they can in the short time remaining to authoritatively inform and educate voters so they can make the most discerning choices possible this coming May.

The emergence of viable anti-establishment candidates is converging with voters' disillusionment with underperforming and disreputable professional, careerist politicians. The thing is, disillusionment can breed incomprehension and lead to indiscriminate decision making.

This disillusionment is not going to go away of its own accord. The educated among the Philippine bodypolitic has its work cut out for them if they hope to stop ignorant voters from making a big mistake. They must leave no stone unturned in developing the sociopolitical consciousness of voters so that those voters will pick the best name to lead the country, not the first convincing candidate they instantly see and hear.

True education and enlightenment are the proven antidotes to voter apathy, fatigue, and regret. Easier said than done, yes. But oh so necessary as time is running out before the May 2016 election.

ooooo

10
Book review of "Two Masters: God or Money"

Dateline, July 27, 2015

**Book: Two Masters: God or Money
(nonfiction)
AUTHOR: Pastor Edmund Danilo Auguis
PUBLISHER: Authorhouse, 187 pages**

In the Book of Matthew in the New Testament, it says that "No man can serve two masters: for either he will hate the one, and love the other; or else he will be devoted to one, and despise the other. You can't serve both God and Mammon [money]." Filipino Pastor Edmund Danilo Auguis of the God Most High Christian Ministry in Great Britain sees the God/Money divide in the same way, which is to say that he is given to prioritizing God over Money despite the vicissitudes of contemporary life that are permeated by the latter.

For a devout Christian this is all fine, but the frequent stresses and immoderate palpitations that can characterize the reality of everyday living might cause even the faith of the most devout to come under greater assault by the requisites of a modern capitalist society. So should we have God stand aside in the name of material necessity (and/or desire) or should He be evoked above everything else?

Pastor Auguis, in what is really a 187-page sermon, sorts this question out. In "Two Masters: God or money," which Auguis presents as a work of admonitory, immutable prose, states that "To trust or worship other gods like mammon [money] is a direct insult and blasphemy to Him because He is the God of everything." Spoken like a true Christian clergyman.

The reader of Auguis's book will soon learn after beginning it that the good pastor doesn't pull his punches in getting to his point of undying lamentation: that our lives are turning more and more on the acquisition and possession of money. As a result, the moral and spiritual sides of those lives are being left hung out to dry. Supporting Auguis's thesis is the profoundly written biblical quote in the Book of Mark, "What does it profit a man if he gains the whole world and loses his soul?"

"Two Masters" is an attempt to convey the foundations of Christian opprobrium for the excesses of capitalism and the covetous attitudes and mindsets it spawns. Auguis employs the Bible and his religious background to thrust forward what he thinks is worth knowing about understanding how to redress what he sees as the imbalance today in the relationship between God and money: "we serve money rather than God."

Auguis does acknowledge the utility and relevance of money. With constant shift of emphases from that concession though, he, with the presence and power of his Christian faith behind him, expands on the theme that the spiritual realm must always take precedence over the realm of money. For Auguis, it is essential that we "not care how much profit we lose as long as we are after the righteousness of God."

Auguis may as well have written in bold letters, "Read the Bible here" in his book since he gives advice about God and Money predominantly from selected biblical quotations and teachings while rarely considering any profane sources. "Two Masters," while very much a worthwhile contribution to the debate at hand, puts the Christian word first before any other thereby rigidly expelling to the sidelines valid non-Christian arguments however comparable.

It goes without saying that Auguis is a Christian pastor so his narrow focus on the Scriptures as the last word on the intemperance of a life centered on money is hardly surprising. But he overestimates the inspirational facility of his faith to seamlessly make the multitudes who are joined at the hip of a modern consumerist society and culture to see the light as he sees it himself when it comes to God and Money. Auguis ends up writing in denial for the ethos of monetary wealth and conspicuous consumerism is written in stone in such a society and culture, so much so that people flout what God or his acolytes have to say in pious disquisition.

Pastor Auguis shows that he is a passionate advocate of a more spiritually enriched and less acquisitive world. But there are far more reasoned narratives to be found in secular humanist circles for what Auguis is depending so much on the Bible to tell us. In short, there are more commonsensically edifying works to turn to in order to understand the

God/Money relationship than Pastor Auguis's sanctimonious and naive treatment of it in "Two Masters."

ooooo

11

Lee Kwan Yew : Discipline Over Democracy in the Philippines

Dateline: 2015

Singaporean statesman Lee Kuan Yew recently passed away at the venerable old age of 91 after years of being situated at the top of Singaporean governance. Sounding eerily like past apologists for authoritarianism, Lee grabbed hold of the autocratic presumption that a great deal of liberal freedom has to be sacrificed for the sake of social order. Lee's Singapore was one such stronghold of that presumption.

In the Philippines, Lee is highly-respected for what he accomplished in tiny Singapore: he transformed a small, third-world island city into an international economic powerhouse. But he is also remembered by Filipinos for his criticisms of their "runaway" democratic system. One of his remarks especially grated on Filipinos. It was one that Lee made in 1992 during a visit to the Philippines. The remark, which was evidently meant for his hosts, was on the precise relation between discipline and democracy and on which was the better choice for any nation: "I believe what a country needs to develop is discipline more than democracy."

I once heard a similar remark from a Philippine army colonel back during the late 1980's when Corazon Aquino was president. When I asked him then why the Philippines was in bad shape and why it was being economically dwarfed by other Southeast Asian neighbors, the colonel painted a picture of a society out of control, a society where disorder and poverty was the norm. The colonel in his infinite wisdom said the reason so many Filipinos were poor was because "they lacked discipline." It was as facile a projection as you could get about Filipinos. Hearing it made my stomach churn with indignation and contempt for this military man who knew next to nothing about the people he had sworn to defend,

Back in the day when Lee Kuan Yew's words were gospel with many policymakers and when the Philippines could not seem to gain its socio-economic long-term footing even under the more reformist Ramos administration, the idea that the lack of discipline was the root cause of the Filipino people's indigence had long been in circulation before Singapore's founding father imparted his authoritarian acumen on the Philippines. I heard many Filipinos themselves express the same sentiment about their fellow countrymen that prosperity would come to them if they could only regulate their behavior and attitudes. It never occurred to these Filipinos that there might be another, more external, more structural explanation as to why their country was an economic straggler.

Lee's pretext of discipline over democracy worked well for Singapore but is thought to be too out of touch with public values in the Philippines. Filipinos are inevitably drawn back to the sugar-coated optimism of having Western-style democratic foundations. Even with features that still require firming up, liberal democracy is a familiar point of origin for Filipinos. Slouching towards an authoritarian system will fail to reconcile Filipinos' democratic compulsions with any definition of socio-political "discipline". If anything, Filipinos have and will continue to resist any permanent plans for anything resembling authoritarian rule.

The tension between discipline (order) and democracy is ultimately a false one in the Philippine context. It is a false dichotomy that has played a central role in the governance of the nation. For decades, the Philippine economic and political elite have envisioned a society that in every last thing order and normality were the rules, rules that fortified their vested, monopolistic interests and which paid lip service to merit and justice. Any democratic and class struggle comers have had to rise against these powerful interests in order to begin to build a fairer and more inclusive state and society.

It is a delicate question as to whether Philippine democracy is a masquerade or the genuine article in practice. We can say that ironically, important democratic principles have been disengaged in the very historical process of implementing Philippine democracy.

Democracy's permanence in the Philippines, with all its ups and downs and its being exploited and manipulated, is open to doubt to the brink of fear and suspicion.

The absence of democracy is something Filipinos vitally learned during the Marcos years. Lee Kuan Yew's suggestion that discipline would solve the Philippines' problems and that Filipinos on all sides should stay away from continuing to roll the dice of democracy is a perception of difference, a perception of difference that doesn't suit the Philippines at all.

Ooooo

12
The SAF Killings
Dateline: 2015

What should the government of Noynoy Aquino do now that the popular anger at the ambush killing of 44 Philippine police Special Action Force (SAF) troops in Mamasapano, Maguindanao province has intensified—and been exploited—to the point that calls for the president's resignation are being felt so keenly? The controversy, deluged as it is in simmering rage, is an inconsolable event for any observer quick to make a default misreading about the perceived inherent treachery of the Moro Islamic Liberation Front (MILF) and by extension, Muslims in general.

By most accounts, it appears there is a strong argument for blaming the absence of proper consultation, communication, judgment, and team integration on everyone immediately involved, from the Philippine government, the National Police (PNP), to the MILF and its "lost command" offshoot, the Bangsamoro Islamic Freedom Fighters (BIFF). Therefore, as might be expected, the tragedy is that at every fateful turn in this case the worst could have been avoided if a modicum of common sense and restraint had been used.

So again, what should the Aquino government do regarding the Mamasapano incident? Thus far, the president has ordered that charges be filed against the responsible parties. That's a reassuring start but what about the overall peace process with the MILF that the administration worked so hard and long for? Should it be rescinded as many outraged Filipino citizens want? Should the administration start beating the drums of war again with the MILF? Under circumstances such as these, it would be a dereliction of duty for the Aquino government to compound the problem by failing to appeal to common sense and erring on the side of caution.

To his credit, Aquino has been one of the quasi-rational voices that have sensibly responded to the killings. He has kept his cool in spite of all the resonating criticism lashing his administration. The president could have easily given in to the overt manifestation of anger emanating from the furthest corners of the country by launching what would be a popular but rash retaliatory blitzkrieg against both the MILF and the BIFF. By acting without acting, Aquino can credibly control the situation and gradually settle the streams of emotions coursing through the bodypolitik without having to take military action which would only inflame tensions.

The moral wrath generated by the killings is charged by the historical link between past atrocities in the Muslim areas of the Philippines and the deep suspicion held for Filipino Muslims. Paralyzed by historical doubt and misrepresentation, Filipinos—like much of the Western world—have marginalized Muslims by identifying them and their religion with terrorism and anti-Christian heresy. Certainly the slaying of the 44 SAF members only magnified that view.

That's why I think it's urgent in this day and age of Islamophobia in non-Muslim societies and violent Islamic extremism in affected parts of the globe to understand that Islam is not a monolithic entity: not every Muslim is a terrorist. Generally-speaking, Muslims all over the world stay in common social alignment with the most temperate interpretation of one of the three great Abrahamic religions. It is only a small minority that has sadistically distorted the message of Islam to the disgust and horror of the vast majority of Muslims.

We would tend to assume that President Aquino—a leader who treats issues with circumspection —is mindful of all this and that is why he will undertake no punitive military action as a result of the Mamasapano clash. Nor should he. At least not against the MILF which has waited too long to conclude and implement a peace deal with the government. The BIFF might be another matter altogether as the group feels that it is being sold out by the MILF. This sets the stage for possible conflict between the BIFF which may very well have conducted the terrible deed, and the central government.

There are now rumors of an impending coup plot against the Aquino administration allegedly due to his "poor" handling of the Mamasapano affair. But no coup is likely to occur; the rumors are probably a gullible stretching of reality by those who are fomenting them. When lined up, the engineered rumors amount to such a sporting scale that the Aquino administration would like to see any potential plotters try it for it is confident that any overthrow attempt will fail absolutely.

Ooooo

13

Pope Francis The Reformer
Dateline: 2015

When Cardinal Jorge Mario Bergoglio was elected pope by a papal conclave in 2013, my first reaction was to ask who was this man who had just ascended to the throne of St. Peter? In order to find out, I started reading about the new Pope Francis to learn as much as I could about him. While the new pope's credentials as a Catholic spiritual leader were impressive, I was disturbed by one particular story that came out of Francis's home country of Argentina.

It was the story of then Cardinal Bergoglio's alleged culpability during Argentina's so-called "dirty war" (ranging from 1974 to 1983) in which the country's military dictatorship is said to have kidnapped and murdered anywhere from 7,000 to 30,000 people who were considered politically-dangerous to the regime. Bergoglio for a time—along with the rest of the Catholic Church in Argentina—had to defend himself against charges of "complicit silence and worse" as the dirty war swirled all around Argentinian society. Bergoglio's purported accountability in the military dictatorship's bloody human rights record remains up for debate. For me, given my loathing for the worst of Vatican hypocrisy and entitlement, it was easy to believe that the man who would be pope could be guilty of turning the other cheek in the face of tyranny and repression aimed at his own people.

However, the allegations have since faded and Pope Francis has established himself as a leader seemingly committed to detaching the Roman Catholic Church from its wayward attitudes and behavior. For a pope who has been a fixture in the Vatican hierarchy, Francis's balancing act between upholding the spiritual legitimacy of the Church and his surprisingly unconventional statements on homosexuality, non-Christians, religion, morality, climate change, and on the Church's financial management, has created the idea that he is not your typical pope; that he will not dogmatically toe the line of encrusted Vatican orthodoxy on certain issues. It is refreshing to hear a papal leader go against the grain of some of his institution's archaic traditions.

It was permanently lodged in my mind that any realistic chance of the Vatican evolving towards greater transparency and reform had been silenced long ago. Pope Benedict XVI gave more lip service than anything else in confronting the corruption within the Vatican, while Pope John Paul II before him did not do much more in dealing with those same problems. What I find encouraging about Pope Francis is that he not only punctuates the plight of the downtrodden on earth but also pontificates on both the excesses of capitalism and on the sins of his own Vatican brethren.

In his official 2014 Christmas gathering with the Vatican hierarchy, Pope Francis forcefully let it be known his highly-critical view of what he called the "15 ailments of the Curia." From self-serving actions to moral hypocrisy and to selling out their spiritual identity for individual gain, Francis fired a warning shot at the stunned Curia audience as he reiterated his commitment to structural reform in the Church and called on the attendees to do some soul-searching into how they have conducted themselves as men of god. It was a marvel to see and hear, and I believe that Francis will do his utmost in fulfilling his lofty goals.

With weary resignation though, I don't expect Francis to be able to turn his reformist plans into concrete results anytime soon. The pope will have to handle any reform effort with care what with the sure resistance of the Vatican curia awaiting him. Perhaps it is little surprise then that Pope Francis could be treading dangerous waters the further he goes into reforming the Church. It's just an unproven conspiracy theory, but it is rumored that Pope John Paul I (the predecessor of the more well-known John Paul II) suddenly died in 1978 after only 33 days in office (officially due to a heart attack) because he was covertly poisoned to prevent his reputed plans to implement reforms in the corruption-ridden Vatican Bank from coming to fruition.

Pope Francis is talking about the doing the same thing Pope John Paul I was thinking of doing. Just pray that Francis's health doesn't abruptly take a turn for the worst any time soon—members of the Vatican curia are capable of doing anything to retain their wealth and power.

Ooooo

14

Death In November
Dateline: Nov. 2013

I wrote this for the FilAm Star in November of 2013. It might have some relevance one year later.

DEATH IN NOVEMBER

Death and November have come together for me like no other month and the grim reaper have before. Fortune has amplified the conjunction of three death events for me, events that occurred during the month of November, the month that doctors say has the greatest likelihood of depression. Two of the events are as public as they come while the third is as private and personal as they come. The first two are the assassination of John F. Kennedy on November 22, 1963 and the natural disaster of Typhoon Haiyan/Yolanda in the Philippines on November 8, 2013. The third is the death of my father which coincidentally, happened the day before one of the worst storms in recent history scuttled the lives of thousands of ill-fated Filipinos.

One thing that all three death events have in common, other than falling in November, is that they were pretty much unexpected. The longer-aged Kennedy Assassination hit the American people out of nowhere, while no one could possibly have predicted with any accuracy of scale the deaths of 5,000-plus Filipinos in the wake of Typhoon Haiyan/Yolanda. The one though, it goes without saying, that will prove most durably extreme in my mind is the death of my father.

The macabre aesthetic of the Kennedy Assassination was the price Americans paid for their illusion of postwar innocence. The greatest murder in modern history awoke Americans to the heart of evil that lies in men, even one of their own. It marked a defiled victory for those responsible for the heinous act and for those who succeeded in covering it up all these years.

It has been a long-standing historical parry to avoid the search for a conspiracy in the Kennedy assassination. But in the light of new credible literature on the subject, it is no longer such a definitive stretch to get a handle on the motives for a conspiracy. The recasting of the assassination from being the responsibility of one lone gunman, Lee Harvey Oswald, to being the paramount concoction of the American Mafia is beginning to gain some traction. After all that has been said and done about JFK's death, it seems likely that the red flag appeal to the conspiratorially-minded will eventually break the containment of conspiracy theories that surround Kennedy's untimely demise.

On the Philippine islands of Leyte and Samar, thousands of Filipinos are being held figurative prisoners by a natural catastrophe and by the incompetence of the central government in Manila. In spite of knowing days ahead of time Super Typhoon Haiyan's projected path through the center of the Philippine archipelago, the administration of Noynoy Aquino has been monumentally ineffectual in its relief efforts for the storm's victims. By the time the Philippine government realized the scope of the calamity on its hands, the impression had gotten across the international community that the Aquino administration was as limp as a dead fish in providing succor and comfort to its distressed citizens in the storm region. One would have expected Philippine officials to have been better prepared but then that would have been too much to ask of this government.

My father arrived in San Francisco from the Philippines at the end of August of this year to undergo throat surgery. Shortly after arriving, he was afflicted with pneumonia which led to multiple organ failure. After several weeks in the ICU and in subacute care, he passed away at the age of 69. I certainly cannot compare my father's death in terms of global magnitude to that of JFK and of the typhoon victims. But I can share the feeling of the transience and tragedy of human life that those who care about JFK and the typhoon victims feel. Whatever we do, whatever we say, whatever we think, there is no way to break with the existential language that we all live by, the language that allows us understand that life is too short and too unpredictable.

In looking back at all three November death events, I wonder what might have been had Kennedy not been assassinated, had 5,000 Filipinos not been snuffed out by Mother Nature, and had my father not died prematurely.What I do know is that their legacies did not expire with their temporal bodies and that we cannot simply say farewell to them without understanding what their existences on earth meant in the greater scheme of things.

ooooo

15
Ninoy Aquino: In Requiem
Dateline: August 2014

What is the definition of a "great man?" For me, it is someone who willingly puts aside their personal safety and interests for a cause that is far greater than themselves. In some cases, they are willing to die for their cause. Several prominent names come immediately to mind: Jesus, Gandhi, Socrates, Martin Luther King Jr., Nelson Mandela, José Rizal.

Based on this criteria, Benigno "Ninoy" Aquino belongs in the "great man" category. True, his killing did not have a major impact on world history as a whole. Plus, Ninoy wasn't always the moral agent that he evolved into towards the end of his life. This shouldn't take anything away however, from the ultimate sacrifice he made for Filipinos.

Ninoy's assassination on August 21, 1983 dramatically altered the reality of the Philippine socio-political scene. His murder galvanized a people that had up until then, given no exceptional grounds for its dictatorial leadership to fear being overthrown by them for the foreseeable future. In the full light of Ninoy's death, Filipinos found the inner strength to begin standing up to the Marcos regime. It would take three more years before the regime was finally deposed in the EDSA I revolt, the genesis of which was sparked by the murderous deed of a ruling clique that had grossly violated the bounds of propriety, legality, and morality.

It is said that historical crises can nourish a person's capacity to mobilize against injustice and tyranny. This is what happened to Ninoy in the period from the start of his banishment to America in 1980 to the moment of his immortalized death. Even in exile and as a recovering heart-surgery patient, Ninoy consistently gave a compelling account of a Philippine administration that was rotting from both within and without. Keeping with the general thrust of his public statements before his martial law arrest in 1972, Ninoy painted a picture of a country being run into the ground by an unholy collection of warlords, sycophants, thieves, and executioners, at the center of which was Ferdinand Marcos.

Ninoy said the time had come for a peaceful transition to democracy in the Philippines. He called on Marcos to leave office before such a transition became untenable, only to have his pleas and warnings fall on deaf ears. The explosive nature of the situation and circumstances ensured that a confrontation between the two men would take place.

Ninoy had undergone a stunning transformation: formerly a cocky, shrewdly-expedient politician and purported womanizer before his incarceration at the hands of Marcos, he emerged from his ordeal a penitent, morally-idealistic, born-again Christian. Ironically it was Ninoy, who as a young provincial governor once said that "a governor is measured, not by the high standards of political morality" but rather by "the actual, physical, material benefits he has brought home to his people."

The ascendancy of the kinder, gentler Ninoy during his exile involved a re-energizing of his love for country and a leap of faith in the workings of a modern democracy. Ninoy felt that the Philippines was caught in an internal struggle "between those who have been mesmerized by the 'efficiency' of authoritarianism and those who still hold that democracy with all its flaws and inefficiency is man's best hope for betterment and progress." For him, there was no doubt as to which system should be adopted and why: "Man's sense of justice makes democracy possible; man's injustice makes it necessary."

If ever there was an episode during Ninoy's renaissance as a human being that has been forever ingrained in my memory, it was not so much the visceral and shocking immediacy of his demise. It was the reported attempt by Imelda Marcos to bribe Ninoy into changing his mind about returning home to help restore Philippine democracy.

Imelda was said to have offered Ninoy a cool $10 million to stay in the US. How easy it would have been for Ninoy to take the money and live comfortably for the rest of his life. It took Ninoy about two seconds to refuse the "gift" of a lifetime. Accepting the money would have meant selling out his conscience, his destiny, his spiritual values, and his people. Ninoy's simple act of altruism in the place of material gain, along with his momentous act of martyrdom, gives us a revealing glimpse of his greatness both as a man and as a Filipino.

ooooo

16
Money Over God
Dateline: July 23, 2014

In a passage in Friedrich Nietzsche's "Thus Spoke Zarathustra", the German philosopher traces the excesses of the modern world to its inevitable consequence. Nietzsche introduced us to one of the most controversial philosophical perceptions of all time: "God is dead." What did he mean by that? One might think that Nietzsche meant God was dead in literal terms. But that's not what he meant at all.

What Nietzsche was trying to say was that we, as modern individuals living in a modern civilization with all its modern forms, norms, and technologies, have metaphorically killed the conception of "God". Our culture of science and secularism has eclipsed what was once an unbreakable faith in a heavenly divinity and has taken its place. What also radically changed social paradigms about religion in modern society was the fast and furious appeal of money and of everything it could purchase and symbolize.

It is the undiluted reality as we live and breathe today: money has supplanted the power and grandeur of God in our hearts and minds. To disabuse those who think this piece is the ranting of a gleefully atheistic nihilist, let us first consider the gap between what we would do for money and material possessions and what we would altruistically do in the name of God. How many of us monetarily capable of doing so would give up substantial amounts of money and material possessions for shall we say, the charitable benefit of the impoverished? I would venture to say that not too many would even if the material sacrifice were of a modest nature and even if the endowment had little effect on their finances.

Despite the outward philanthropy and compassion articulated by many of the Christian faithful, the truth is far too many of them cannot practice what they preach or what they profess to believe in. The philosopher G. K. Chesterton came close to the point I am trying to make. He once said "The Christian ideal has not been tried and found wanting; it has been found difficult and left untried." Chesterton laid bare the chasm between the Christian ideal and the conducting of a wholehearted effort to meet that ideal.

Many self-proclaimed Christians are misguided in believing that by merely going through the motions of the core Christian rituals (attending mass, constant prayers, taking communion, going to confession, etc.) that they are being good Christians. But are they being good Christians when they exhibit the proper religious observances on the surface but flout the ideals of Christianity in their actions? I argue that going to mass, saying your prayers, taking communion, and going to confession is the easy part of being a Christian. Anyone can perform these formalities with the same amount of effort that is required to turn on the television. However, the hard part is actually behaving and functioning as morally compassionate and conscientious Christians.

This contradiction is especially highlighted when the question of money comes up. We have become not only a society, but a world of extravagant consumer appetites and desires. We are a world of material accumulation and possessiveness in which deified brand names and fetishized status symbols such as cars, houses, clothes, and bank accounts come to be the pivotal assets that determine who is good or bad, who is right or wrong, and who is superior or inferior.

Christianity as it is observed today doesn't match the traditional idea of how it is supposed to be observed. Although in all fairness being a Christian can be challenging and sometimes unbearable in our modern society. In today's universal framework of money and materialism, it might be too much to ask for Christians to be Christians. That doesn't mean they cannot try harder in acting like they are really adhering to the teachings of their faith, rather than deluding themselves into thinking they are acting like Christians when in fact they are simply fulfilling on a barebones scale what is expected of them from their Christian upbringing and culture.

I am tired of seeing human relationships and humanity in general suffer terribly because we have traded our spiritual and moral identities, Christian or otherwise, in exchange for a material one. Nietzsche saying that God is dead is one way of describing this polarizing path. Selling your soul to the devil is another.

Ooooo

17
Russia, Crimea, China and the Philippines
Dateline: April 21, 2014

Russia's incursion into Ukraine's Crimean peninsula has the same kinds of portents for the Philippines as it reacts to China's geostrategic claims and dictations in the South China Sea. There is no contradiction in drawing parallels between these two separate issues, issues which are half a world apart. One hegemonic power (Russia) has taken it upon itself to occupy the region of another country (Ukraine). Who is to say that another hegemonic power (i.e. China) would not, under the right circumstances, do the same to smaller nations such as the Philippines?

Throughout history, powerful countries and civilizations have felt the urge to dominate their weaker neighbors. The Southeast Asian countries of Vietnam, Malaysia, Indonesia, and the Philippines certainly feel that way about China which has been accused of regional intimidation as it asserts its territorial prerogatives in the South China Sea. These acts of intimidation on the part of China have increased over the last few years and are bound to bring rival claimants in the region to an impossible choice: either cave in to Beijing's claims or be prepared to go to war over them.

Despite the Philippine government's protests against Chinese intimidation and incursion in the disputed Spratly Islands in the South China Sea, Beijing's military presence continues to haunt the region. Let us not kid ourselves: China's growing presence is not going to go away anytime soon, nor will it be easily alleviated by diplomacy and compromise. The fact of the matter is that Beijing wants all of the Spratlys, not just some of them. What the Philippine government should take away from Beijing's attitude is that it will eventually have to make the tough decision between giving its giant neighbor what it wants and in the process leave itself open to accusations of appeasement, or remain steadfast in resisting China at the risk of conflict.

So far, the government of Noynoy Aquino has chosen a middle path between these two extremes: the path of rhetorically standing up to Beijing in the media and in diplomatic circles but also simultaneously avoiding direct confrontation with it. The Aquino administration's pragmatic stance is understandable but may prove to be costly down the road. Look at the United States' and Western Europe's tactfully incremental approach towards expanding NATO eastward in Europe over the last 20 years. The expansion is proving to be, despite the organization's best intentions, an iniquitously thorny issue for Russia which sees the expansion as a growing threat to its security. The expansion sowed the seeds for Moscow's Anschluss of Ukraine's Crimean peninsula. By the same token, the import of Manila's currently subtle actions regarding China and the South China Sea may not have as much meaning now as they will have in the future.

It's a risky proposition no doubt, but the Philippines will have to at some point, show some real spine in defending its territorial rights against China lest the Middle Kingdom run roughshod over them the way Russia has done over Ukrainian land. I fear that the Aquino government has been tepid in responding to Chinese incursions in the Spratlys, particularly when it comes to areas which are legally under Philippine sovereignty. This is not to say that Manila should precipitously seek war with China. Diplomacy, no matter how difficult and ultimately unlikely to succeed as it is, is still the preferred option on both sides of the issue no matter what the hawks in Beijing say. But constantly stepping on eggshells to avoid China's wrath is no stance at all and can be said to be a cowardly one. Some of those disputed islets are according to international norms, part of the Philippines. Therefore, it is the duty of the Aquino government to defend Philippine sovereignty over them.

Even as China has deigned to grace the South China Sea with its ominous presence, the outgunned and outsized government in Manila can be rest assured that it has a real ace up its sleeve that Beijing has to be wary of before it decides it can run rampant over the area. That ace is the United States which is treaty-bound to come to the defense of the Philippines if its territory is attacked. Having said that, that option presages a frightening situation in which two nations with hundreds of nuclear weapons would confront each other with 100 million Filipinos caught in the middle.

ooooo

18
Remembering Pork Barrel
Dateline: Feb. 26, 2014

I hope I'm wrong about this, but I'm getting an intuitive sense that the collective shock and anger caused by the Pork Barrel fiasco is beginning to fade a tad. Someone please tell me that this isn't so and that it's just a matter of my being prematurely pessimistic. Although I lack any expert consensus on the matter, I fear that Filipinos are ever so slightly shifting their attention away from one of the most egregious fiduciary misappropriations in Philippine political history. And that's saying a lot considering the Philippines' long history of politically-induced fiduciary misappropriations.

A lot of Filipinos picture the Pork Barrel scam in two ways: there are those who see it as a form of moral turpitude that should never be excused under any circumstances; and then there are those who inform their judgment of the scandal with a combination of waning outrage and measured standards about the innocence or guilt of the accused.

It is due to this that we can detect the smatterings of compounded diffidence among once-indignant Filipinos. If on the mark, some would say that this would confirm that the so-called Filipino value of "ningas cogon" is rearing its head again in the face of the latest political and financial transgression that has been thrust upon Filipinos. "Ningas Cogon" summed up, refers to Filipinos' alleged tendency not to finish what they've started. Like the type of grass that it is named after, ningas cogon reflects the purported Filipino pattern of coming out on fire at the beginning but then burning out like a flash in the pan.

Some very proud Filipinos would regard ningas cogon as an unfair characterization of themselves. But let's look at part of the record over the past quarter century: none of the Marcoses have been punished for their crimes against the Filipino people and they are in fact planning a political comeback; Joseph Estrada was pardoned for his executive corruption and then elected Manila mayor; Gloria Macapagal-Arroyo continues to stave off true incarceration by staying in an innocuous state of hospital arrest, all the while serving as a congresswoman; numerous politicians in both the House of Representative and the Senate who are strongly suspected of corruption and other felonies remain in office. How could all of this have transpired if the voters were active and vigilant as they should have been?

Ninotchka Rosca wrote in her 1988 novel, "State of War," that the Philippines is "a country of beginnings." She is right about Filipinos always willing to light the fire of change and evolution, but do they have the staying power to see the process through to its conclusion? Anyone trying to write mostly in a sanguine chord here can go on the record as appearing hopeful and optimistic about Filipinos. Fine, more power to these indigenous particularists. But "ningas cogon" captures the truth about a lot of Filipinos, that their first and last instinct is to cling to immediacy, that they---and this perhaps is human nature---wallow in anger and outrage at the outset only to squander the power that discontented emotion can generate and lose it to the multitude of banal demands that everyday life imposes on them.

Everybody knows with a fair degree of accuracy that certain parties were all but caught red-handed in ripping off the pork barrel fund of millions of dollars, not just pesos. What I want to know is this: are Filipinos little more than a bunch of "beginners" who will give in to impatience and frustration with the drawn-out nature of the pork barrel scam and therefore find "better" things to do with their lives? As the storm of the scandal hits lulls of public attention, it becomes too easy for Filipinos to grow weary of the whole mess, which is exactly what the politicians in question want. The Estradas, the Revillas, Enrile, and other indicted individuals are stalling for time, hoping that the longer the scandal drags on, the more likely public attention will fall off.

This article is my way of calling out those Filipinos who are standing apathetically on the sidelines or who are losing interest. If you think what I wrote here is wrong, then prove it by not letting go of the Pork Barrel scam until justice has been done to the perpetrators.

ooooo

\

19
Pork Barrel Scandal
Dateline: Oct. 2, 2013

The Pork Barrel scandal that is currently roiling Philippine politics offers a penetrating glimpse into how public funds have been nefariously used in the past for anything but the Philippine public. The scandal though, at the center of which is businesswoman Janet Lim-Napoles, offers more than a revealing view of the Byzantine treatment that is applied to pecuniary items like the Priority Development Assistance Fund (PDAF). It pulls out from the dark the sustained trend among Philippine politicos of misappropriating substantive amounts of public finances in order to line their pockets.

Filipino politicians stealing from public coffers is hardly news. The march of graft and corruption by elected officials has tempered into a perverse tradition, something to be expected of any politician made of flesh and blood. While it has been a popular refrain among Filipinos to curse politicians from all corners of the political spectrum for stealing what belongs to the people, the absurdity of it all is that Filipinos have been tangibly bland or resigned to fate in acting on their abhorrence to being royally shafted by their leaders.

When the PDAF scandal first broke, Filipinos knew they would have to brace themselves for yet another harmful shock to the democratic system. The thinking was: here we go all over again. Politicians dipping their hands in the till---when has it never happened? Philippine history, haphazardly packaged and articulated as it is in a knotted reign of domestic and international designs, tells us that politicians big and small show little life in formulating and passing progressive legislation but bring it on when easy blood money is at hand.

Many indifferently or arrogantly thought, first among them the censurable politicians, that Filipinos would do as they usually do: turn the other cheek and worry more about the sobering realm of everyday life. But as the tune goes, there's something happening here. The tinder of corruption that these crooked politicians now find piled up underneath them has been set alight by the piercing anger of the people. Is it a sign of how minds in the Philippines are changing for the better? Hard to say for certain, but maybe it's not totally unreasonable to believe that the bad guys won't get away with it this time.

Rarely over the many years since the Philippines gained its independence from America in 1946 has it come close to realizing its potential as a democratic republic. Since the American flag came down on July 4, 1946, the country has been sucked dry by staggering economic inequality and its attendant mix of poverty, mismanagement, and corruption. Most misleading about all this is the economic and political establishment's perpetual assertion that it is the lack of order and discipline among the people, as well as the presumed Filipino penchant for indolence, that has always brought the Philippines to this sorry state of affairs.

But this curious contention on the part of the economic and political elite crosses the line of incredulity. Indeed, nothing could be farther from the truth. The reason the Philippines has been so poor for so long is not because of the underprivileged, but because of the rich who constitute much of the upper rungs of the economic and political hierarchy. Seeking to capitalize on the blame-the-poor ditch of responsibility, the economic and political elite shovel falsehoodsabout the wider Filipino society in order to convince the masses that it's their own fault that the Philippines is being driven off a cliff.

The elite has built their wealth and power on this myth which has been useful in getting Filipinos to suppose that there has never really been any money available for the improvement of the country. This flight of fancy conceals what is a distorted fact of history: there has always been sufficient funds in the Philippines for social and economic growth and development; but those funds have been heisted on a socio-historical terrain that has been branded by the problem of massive economic criminality.

In so many ways, the emergence of the pork barrel scandal is salutary for the Philippine nation and people. I just hope Filipinos have the staying power to pursue the brazen thieves who populate the institutions of state, lest we continue to put the fate of the Philippines in the hands of these political and moral charlatans.

Ooooo

20
Juan Ponce Enrile's Memoir:
A Critical Review
Dateline: Sept. 10, 2013

Former Philippine Defense Minister Juan Ponce Enrile is almost 90 now. Given his advanced age, it's understandable that Enrile would want to strike an autobiographical pose and finally tell his life story in his own, differentiated and protean eloquence. However, Richard Nixon once said that it would depend on who is writing the history in response to the question of how he would be ultimately judged by historians. But when the subject himself is the author, his narcissistic entitlement to protect his image obviously must be factored in Nixon's perspicacious treatment of personal historiography.

This is especially true of contemporary public figures whose opponents have preached their downfall for a litany of high crimes. Juan Ponce Enrile has never been able break out of the moral and ethical chains that his detractors have tried to bring him down with from the height of power and influence he once stood on. But that hasn't stopped the former defense minister and confidant of Ferdinand Marcos from attempting to piously soar above his direct culpability in the Marcos dictatorship and live the life of a respected, elder statesman.

My first reaction to the publication of "Juan Ponce Enrile: A Memoir" was that the defense minister and former senator's words, remarks, genuflections, and reprise of his self-imagined role as patriot and moral guide would not escape his remarkable facility for generating controversy. I hate to say I told you so, but I told you so. This more than 800-page tome of a memoir, if you look past the author's unconcealed alacrity in sharing intimate details about his life from the time he was born, caters more to those inclined to vindicate Enrile's actions as defense minister during the Philippines' slide into martial law than to those who saw the man for what he really was: a crassly self-serving, ministerial autocrat, a political manipulator of the highest grade, a monopolistic plunderer of national treasure, and a dominant and ruthless figure during Ferdinand Marcos's martial law regime.

Over the years, there has been enough meaningful evidence to at least warrant an organized, mainline investigation into Enrile's conduct during the martial law years. To the great extent to which he was a key subject in the Marcos regime, Enrile is alleged---not without basis---to have enriched himself at the country's expense and to have taken great pains in facilitating the incarceration, sometimes the elimination, of the regime's opponents. That he was more than in a fair position of power to do what he is accused of only makes it that much more unpalatable and outrageous that Enrile has approached his future requiem of a memoir with all the irreproachability and innocence he can muster.

To the good Filipinos whose lives were repressed by martial law, the added burden of swallowing Enrile's distorted balance sheet of responsibility is too much to ask for. The victims of martial law deserve better than they have gotten. Enrile has done them absolutely no favor in suppressing history for the sake of posterity and for the benefit of his own millstone legacy.

Is Enrile strictly writing his long-awaited memoir as a prejudicial cultivation of his self-portrait or out of a primal fear that the sands of time are running out for him and that he must express some noble sentiments and helpful commentary while he still can, before the furies of oblivion can transport him to the land of just desserts? The probable answer is both: Enrile is whitewashing his public past in a considered appeal not only to the derivations of public opinion but also to the deferment of a celestial justice.

Thus inspired, Enrile has perceptibly overstretched his unlimited appetite for frequently imagining Philippine socio-political history over the last forty years on his own sustained terms. To the point, Enrile has up until now gotten away with casting his offenses out of the social consciousness and into the dustbin of history. It's a tad ironic though that his memoir, the memoir that was supposed to settle his accounts with history and with the victims of martial law, has reopened the proverbial can of worms that is Enrile's overt and covert record as defense minister.

Indeed, there is much opprobrium, great and small, in his known file that catches the circumspect eye. With an extreme emphasis on that shamelessly sinister account of his professional career, "Juan Ponce Enrile: A Memoir" as far as moral documents go, isn't worth the paper it's printed on.

ooooo

21
Nonoy Aquino's 30th Death Anniversary: In Retrospect
Dateline: April 21, 2013

What is the definition of a "great man?" For me, it is someone who willingly puts aside their personal safety and interests for a cause that is far greater than themselves. In some cases, they are willing to die for their cause. Several prominent names come immediately to mind: Jesus, Gandhi, Socrates, Martin Luther King Jr., Nelson Mandela, José Rizal.

Based on this criteria, Benigno "Ninoy" Aquino belongs in the "great man" category. True, his killing did not have a major impact on world history as a whole. Plus, Ninoy wasn't always the moral agent that he evolved into towards the end of his life. This shouldn't take anything away however, from the ultimate sacrifice he made for Filipinos.

Ninoy's assassination on August 21, 1983 dramatically altered the reality of the Philippine socio-political scene. His murder galvanized a people that had up until then, given no exceptional grounds for its dictatorial leadership to fear being overthrown by them for the foreseeable future. In the full light of Ninoy's death, Filipinos found the inner strength to begin standing up to the Marcos regime. It would take three more years before the regime was finally deposed in the EDSA I revolt, the genesis of which was sparked by the murderous deed of a ruling clique that had grossly violated the bounds of propriety, legality, and morality.

It is said that historical crises can nourish a person's capacity to mobilize against injustice and tyranny. This is what happened to Ninoy in the period from the start of his banishment to America in 1980 to the moment of his immortalized death. Even in exile and as a recovering heart-surgery patient, Ninoy consistently gave a compelling account of a Philippine administration that was rotting from both within and without. Keeping with the general thrust of his public statements before his martial law arrest in 1972, Ninoy painted a picture of a country being run into the ground by an unholy collection of warlords, sycophants, thieves, and executioners, at the center of which was Ferdinand Marcos.

Ninoy said the time had come for a peaceful transition to democracy in the Philippines. He called on Marcos to leave office before such a transition became untenable, only to have his pleas and warnings fall on deaf ears.

The explosive nature of the situation and circumstances ensured that a confrontation between the two men would take place.

Ninoy had undergone a stunning transformation: formerly a cocky, shrewdly-expedient politician and purported womanizer before his incarceration at the hands of Marcos, he emerged from his ordeal a penitent, morally-idealistic, born-again Christian. Ironically it was Ninoy, who as a young provincial governor once said that "a governor is measured, not by the high standards of political morality" but rather by "the actual, physical, material benefits he has brought home to his people."

The ascendancy of the kinder, gentler Ninoy during his exile involved a re-energizing of his love for country and a leap of faith in the workings of a modern democracy. Ninoy felt that the Philippines was caught in an internal struggle "between those who have been mesmerized by the 'efficiency' of authoritarianism and those who still hold that democracy with all its flaws and inefficiency is man's best hope for betterment and progress." For him, there was no doubt as to which system should be adopted and why: "Man's sense of justice makes democracy possible; man's injustice makes it necessary."

If ever there was an episode during Ninoy's renaissance as a human being that has been forever ingrained in my memory, it was not so much the visceral and shocking immediacy of his demise. It was the reported attempt by Imelda Marcos to bribe Ninoy into changing his mind about returning home to help restore Philippine democracy.

Imelda was said to have offered Ninoy a cool $10 million to stay in the US. How easy it would have been for Ninoy to take the money and live comfortably for the rest of his life. It took Ninoy about two seconds to refuse the "gift" of a lifetime. Accepting the money would have meant selling out his conscience, his destiny, his spiritual values, and his people. Ninoy's simple act of altruism in the place of material gain, along with his momentous act of martyrdom, gives us a revealing glimpse of his greatness both as a man and as a Filipino.

Ooooo

22
Philippine Elections 2013
Dateline: June 4, 2013

Love them or hate them, one thing never changes about elections in the Philippines: they are packaged as the practice of a deep and welcoming democracy. Welcoming that is, to the waves of the Philippine masses, the common folk of the country upon whom Philippine democracy is supposed to be founded on.

But the term "democracy" is used in different countries to mean different things. The tumult of democracy as we come across it in the Philippines is stocked with charitable rhetoric woven with promises for the people, promises that flow into the social consciousness as important talking points that will one day ring with the sound of gainful consummation for anyone and everyone. This rhetoric soon gives way though to familiar political terrain, to terrain where progressive change becomes the vernacular currency of the day but then is explained away as being impractical, untimely, or just not worth talking about anymore.

Things have to change for them to stay the same. So the saying goes. It is a tried-and-true alignment in Philippine politics and society. Like many of their predecessors, the newly-elected solons to the Philippine Senate know how to talk up a storm about presuming to be champions of the masses and political phoenixes rising from the ashes of socio-political apathy and economic drift, as well as personifications of national unity with the Filipino people.

A reality check is needed here: once you escape the abject bubble of smiling, inviolate imagery and appealing name and face recognition, you might reasonably ask what this scathing portrait is before you. It is a spine-shivering portrait of what is no longer one of the most honorable institutions of the land. From top to bottom you can pick out at least half dozen individuals who have no intellectual or ethical right to be in the senate, let alone run in a campaign for it.

In the pairing of the Philippine electoral process with the disconsolate principle of primarily voting for the most fashionable and recognizable candidates---instead of the most qualified ones---Philippine elections have been preserved as token objects of democratic legitimacy. It is an electoral precondition that Filipino voters are allowed a chance to express their political free will through the instrument of the election. Instead, what really gets expressed are populist projections of support for unscrupulous, opportunistic, stage managed candidates who seldom represent the best interests of the people.

The voters' blind fervor for candidates who patronize the exercise of their political rights strengthens the rule of the powerful and wealthy in the Philippines. The last time I looked, this socio-political state of affairs was called an oligarchy. To their minds at least, if they have to pick a bunch of life-sized oligarchs for office, then Filipinos are free to pick their own along with the oligarchs' sons and daughters. In Philippine politics, dynastic blood is thicker than the free and fair ballot. By modern standards, this is not even a democracy variant. The only way to identify this sobering hyphenization of democracy as anything but anti-democratic is to wake up each morning and to tell yourself that the sun came up because it revolves around the earth.

Really now, what are the newly-elected senators going to do that will be any different from what their inept and hypocritical predecessors did? Will these kindred souls do anything to alleviate poverty? Will they be the bane of dirty, corrupt, self-serving politicos? Will this hand-picked group of twelve continue to play their likely roles of public underachievers who won't dare rock the boat? If history is to be any indicator, then Filipino voters, because of their benighted choices, have unwittingly helped undermine Philippine democracy.

Politicians in a democracy are supposed to take on their constituents' general vision of things, their riveting dreams, their visceral fears, their suitably sized universe of plans and intentions. But in the treacherously real world of Philippine political history and culture, this democratic expectation is poison for entitled, self-seeking politicians who currently fill the Philippines' legislative branch with their hot air and grating unconcern.

It wasn't hard to be discontented with the latest charade of a national election in the Philippines. Some of the political faces may have changed, but the lethargic, dismissive spirit remains among the senators both new and old. As I said before, things must change in order for them to remain the same.

ooooo

23
Xmas Article
December 28, 2009

As is always the case in the twelfth hour of the old year and in the advent of the new, people ride high on elevated expectations, expectations that cut to the dawn of a new beginning, to the potential for positive developments in their lives, and to the hope of a spiritual epiphany that will put them at ease in a worldly existence that is increasingly becoming more cynical as we speak. Whether this sanguinity is based on accurate thinking or on a delusionary detachment from reality is hardly the point. What is important here is that by waxing optimistically, we manage to deal with life's great challenges, challenges that tyrannize people's commonplace lives in every society on the globe.

Many of us wish we could be living in better times. What I mean by better times should not necessarily translate into financial status. What I mean by better times also relates to a life where we live in harmony with nature, with the community of mankind, with our friends and families, and with our inner being.

In many ways, this is the story of Filipinos and Filipino Americans today. It is a story of material greed, pride, and selfishness. It is also the story of human compassion and understanding unspoiled by brazen self-interest, crass politicization, or profit-mongering. More suggestive of this story is how God has been circulated in the equation of the particular reality that has descended on Filipinos and FilAms. The notion of not believing in God is so alien to Filipino Christians that they are unable to de-link their lives from the concept of a higher power. For these Filipinos, God is the ultimate refuge from the cares and stresses of modern existence. They mythicize God's incarnation in the sacred texts of Christianity as the Word that permeates their hearts and minds. The Word inspires these Filipinos to look forward to the future, to fill their lives with a powerful set of meanings, to compose an edifying vocabulary by which they act upon their aspirations and succinctly represent the essence of their self-identity.

But God is also noticeable from his perceived absence in the lives of other Filipinos. These Filipinos tend to be agnostics if not outright atheists. They would rather stand in the cold glare of the temporal world rather than in the chimerical warmth of what they believe to be a hollow religion. These more profane Filipinos read their lives and the world around them convinced that truth and knowledge are revealed through rational illumination rather than through divine revelation.

Between God up above and rational man down on earth, who does the best job of making a difference in how we face the risks and challenges that can make or break us? The core debate is not much different now than it was five hundred years ago.

What has changed is the historical context. We are presently informed by a hyper-capitalistic culture in a society that is not done putting the finishing touches on the worst economic downturn since the Great Depression.

Of course, it is always possible to read too much into how deeply economic conditions can skew people's states of mind. Being in financial distress however, as so many Filipinos and FilAms are in nowadays, can bewilder a person's attitude towards life. This is where the grace of God or man's rational ability to cope with the slings and arrows of modern existence comes in.

Trying to survive today is like walking through an endless hall of mirrors strewn with traps and pitfalls. Anxiety and sometimes, animosity, are the result. In working our way through these feelings as individuals trapped in an economic recession, we not only try to get past the painful present, but head for what has to be a rosier future. We try to make sense of all this by entreating the heavens or by contemplating our human selves.

There are times when spiritual faith and human reason are crowded out by the exigencies of everyday life. But that shouldn't stop us from being able to appreciate what should be most important to us: our physical health, our emotional well-being, our loved ones, and our fellow human beings. If we take proper stock of our lives, beyond the arenas of material pursuits and possessions, the wonderful possibilities they contain will eventually manifest themselves for those deserving of them.

Ooooo

24
Beaches
No date

I am walking along Ocean Beach at land's edge with the Pacific surf nipping at my heels. As I stroll southward along the beach, I watch the sun take its diurnal dive over the horizon, leaving in its wake a pink, bluish cast to the fading light that clings to the Western sky. It is thoroughly enchanting, this exquisite, elegiac scene of the Sun's death being played out before me. But there is something else, equally alluring as the sun, drawing my attention.

My eyes are averted to my left side a nd I see cars speeding along the Great Highway, trying to race the ocean tides and the omnipresent seagulls overseeing the beach. A sluggish melancholy overtakes me, as the sense of wistful contentment that I reapedfrom enjoying the Sun's demise abruptly disappears with the noise of the automobiles screeching by. Darkness has just come, enhancing the aura of the lights on the Great Highway. Standing on the grimy beach with sand crunching in my shoes, I try to look up at the newly born night sky, searching for some visible body that will remind me how insignificant I am compared to the infinite totality of theuniverse.

It is a typically chilly evening, but the chronic Northern California fog has chosen to stay away this night, clearing the heavens for almost perfect viewing. Still, I lose my bearings looking for Venus, the brightest star and a planet whose remote beauty gleams like a benediction in my soul. But I am looking in the wrong place. The brightest object is not in the night sky, but is adjacent to the Great Highway in the form of a huge neon light outlining the American flag, sparkling brilliantly against the background of the black Pacific Ocean. Placed there in memory of the September 11 tragedy, the flag-light is as allegorical as it is partisan, representative as it is dazzling, revealing as it is stylized.

The electronic flag serves as a glorified dust jacket, a dust jacket that begins to convey what the phenomenon that is America is about. In looking at the electronic monstrosity before me, I see in my mind's eye a representation of a nation beset by free and creative winds generated by its tolerant and generous inhabitants. I see a nation that is enamored by the bliss of individualism and by the wonders technological progress.

And I see a nation invested by the vagaries of God, by the grandeur ofdisproportionate power, by the bewitchery of glistening icons, and by the colorof violence and money. Having lived in America since I was one year of age, I have come to the conclusion that it is a republic running vigorously in stride,but with long shadows crossing overhead.

I have shed tears of joy living in America, having read, witnessed, and experienced how breathtaking and extraordinary this great country can be. At the same time, I have shed tears of anger and sorrow at how inequitable it has been for so many. America troubles me the way I become unsettled when I read Dostoyevsky or a Shakespearean tragedy. I shudder in suspense at what awaits me on the next page, but not unlike a famished lover who thinks he or she knows a good thing when they see one, I keep reading on to the very end. Despite being bowled over by the effulgence of the light- flag, as well as by the symbolism it imparted, I resume my walk southward along the beach. As I try to gather my thoughts, I shift my gaze irresistibly at what I can still observe of the dark Pacific in all its churning, restless immensity. My gaze stretches thousands of leagues to the Philippines, the land of my birth. I can't bear to contemplate how far away it really is. I fool myself into thinking that the Philippine archipelago is just over the horizon, that all I have to do to get there is take a small boat and cruise for no more than a few minutes to the point where the ocean meets the sky. There, I will see the contours of palm trees, of soaring and rutted mountains, together with the perfect cone that is Mayon volcano.

I will feast my eyes on the celebrated steps of Banaue's rice terraces and on the metropolitan buildings that line Manila's Roxas Boulevard facing Manila Bay. I will eagerly discern the vivid colors belonging to brown-olive bodies, green dense-as-can-be jungles, and gaudy smoke-emitting jeepneys, not to mention the bright red blood shed by a rooster in a cockfight. There are also the rusted colors of corrugated roofs covering the dilapidated dwellings that poor Filipinos call home, and the multihued chromaticity of the sails attached to the bancas that are coming out to meet me. I will smell the luscious aroma of lechon kawali, kare kare, and of pancit canton wafting through the atmosphere. I will taste the sweet, delectable taste of halo halo, lecheflan, and of the santol fruit. And I will feel the heat, that oppressive, tropical heat and humidity that mercilessly engulfs the anatomy of this cold-acclimated Californian.

I am mesmerized now, floating in an alchemy of harmony and promise. The Philippines awaits me, its possibilities endless under a pearly, cerulean expanse or beneath a razor-sharp crescent moon. It offers me the balance and proportion and adventure that America cannot. But the Philippines is an apparition, an abstraction, a terra incognita, something that I cannot touch or comprehend as a miniscule figure on the distant, opposite side. Stretching my imagination across the ocean depths is not enough to make me forget that there is no substitute for being there. Yet, I am left to ponder a surreal image in my mind, an enduring image that is wondrous, spiritual, and at once, anguished. It is an image of the Philippines, the land where I, as a prematurely sentimental teenager hurriedly searching for his roots, once wanted to be laid to rest as soon as I could stop having to mark the passage of time and cease renewing my life's meaning.

Here is the image I am projecting: I am still walking on a beach, but this one is covered with immaculate white sand, gently buffeted with balmy breezes. The water lapping on the beach is crystal-clear, tepid, teeming with tiny forms of life swimming around my feet. Exotic birds, radiant creatures of flight that only God's boundless originality could have conceived, dart among the foliage and soar above the beach, sounding their hymns from their pulpits on the ground and in the air. Chocolate-skinned children run up and down the beach, speaking a Babel of tongues, splashing water at each other and rollicking in the tender waves. It is high noon, and the Sun's rays are burning into my skin, making the sand pleasantly warm and my body shiny with perspiration.

The centerpiece of the beach is a narrow, hollowed out vertical piece of rock, measuring about six feet high and situated a few steps from the shore. Contained within it is a life-sized statue of the Virgin Mary. It is bizarrely surrounded by strobe lights which flash at night and cause the statue to appear to be moving slightly within its half-opened rocky niche. The Virgin is a revered figure in the Philippines. She embodies the ideals of moral purity and spiritual devotion that Filipino Cchristians strive to attain. She also acts as a savior for millions of Filipinos. The Virgin is their redeemer, their protector, and their guide for they are lost and alienated in their own home, in their own country.

I wait for night to fall before I move closer to the statue. Some of the native inhabitants try to dissuade me from approaching the Virgin. Leave her be in peace and do not transgress what should not be transgressed, they appeal. But I choose to ignore them, dismissing their admonitions as medieval superstition. It is not my intention to sacrilegiously violate the Virgin's threshold.

I simply want to see her up close because from a distance she is beautiful, vibrant, and blessed. I have this irresistible desire to touch her, to feel her piety and spiritual energy running through me.

Standing directly in front of the Virgin, I examine her, awed by her chastity and benevolence. The strobe lights have been switched on in the meantime, making the statue appear extraordinarily natural. So natural in fact, that I notice the Virgin is scrutinizing the constellations on high. Perhaps she is empathizing with God while doingso.

Suddenly, she looks at me with crimson-tinted orbs. The Virgin has been weeping in silence, fine threads of tears streaming down her vestal countenance. In this moment of passionate intensity, I somehow come to understand that she is crying for the Filipino people, for their sufferings, for their mutilated hopes, for the annihilation of their innocence, and for the forgiveness of sins that they had been forced to commit.

Bewildered, my rational mind struggles to come to grips with this instance of divine revelation. Everything in the rational ethos, indeed the American ethos, that I have learned, been subjected to, and engaged in since I can remember tells me that I only fantasized the sight of the statue crying. We all see what we want to see, so say the full-blown acolytes of callous American rationality. But the burgeoning traces of my Filipino genesis grants me no reprieve from the phantoms of my cultural visions. The Virgin was crying and will always be crying as far as the Philippines is concerned.

American rationality is inappropriate in this context. As such, it is a perishable product, its heaped-up ideas and concepts of logic, profit, and science having been shattered on the tempered wall of spiritual faith. Render onto God what is God's. Render onto America what is America's.

I used to coerce myself into believing that the Philippines was my real homeland, the true gravitational field of my ethnic and cultural self, of my solicitous heart, and of my esteemed and infamous pedigree. I bore this mask despite the fact that the United States was where I was raised and educated to be a compliant little citizen, brandishing his blue passport at anyone questioning my right to genuflect under the triumphal arch of all that America stands for.

But for a time, I could not stomach America's arrogance and condescension, its backdoor politics, selective morals, schizophrenic notions of freedom and order, obsession with capital, and its almighty power to speak for others. My disillusionment was such that I would regulate my use of English so that I would not sound too fluent when conversing with Tagalog-speakers. My purpose was to avoid giving the impression that I was dreadfully "spoken in dollar." In other words, as a Filipino American, I was scared to death of Filipinos perceiving me as being too American and not very Filipino—a turning of the Filipino colonial mentality on its head. Quite a contradiction: that I would pretend I was not a child of America, when in truth I was, first and foremost, a creation of it.

I have changed for the better I think, since those giddy days of pretense and guises. I am no longer ashamed to call English my mother tongue. No longer am I mortified to be unable to hold even the simplest conversation in Tagalog. Rather than depending on sleights of hand, embellishments, and alibis to reinforce a half-identity, I have found a comfort zone of sorts, between my modern American nurturing and my primal Filipino origins. Paradoxically speaking, I belong to neither culture and to both. I belong to neither Ocean Beach in San Francisco or to that mystical, whitewashed strand of equatorial coastline, located somewhere and anywhere in the Philippines, that haunts my reveries. All the same however, both points serve as signposts that show me the right path whenever I stray into the impenetrable thicket of cultural anonymity and confusion.

To complete the image: the Virgin is not crying or looking at me any longer. She has reverted back to her previous stance, a taut, yet flowing posture etched in deep repose. But for me, the image as a whole has taken on a new form, a form that I have trouble fathoming as the two beaches blur into an amorphous heap of hazy visualizations and sensations. I can barely distinguish them in that state.

Perplexed and exhausted, I sit down on the sand sliding beneath me and try to digest what has just happened. Before I can solve the puzzle, two miniature angels alight onto my shoulders. The Filipino angel on my left shoulder is excitedly nodding its head up and down in praise, while the American angel on my right shoulder is cynically shaking its head sideways in repudiation. Desperate for answers, I plead to the Virgin for intercession. Just as she is about to speak, the Virgin squelches the words before they can escape from her mouth. She smiles at me instead. With that smile, in that fleeting nanosecond of illuminating quietude, I must say that everything became absolutely clear tome.

ooooo

25
Democracy Versus Discipline

Dateline, July 28, 2008

Discipline, discipline, discipline. It's the lack of discipline stupid. That in a nutshell, is why the Philippines is in the state that it is in today. This is according to Filipinos and Filipino Americans who foster the notion that their suffering countrymen and women back home are apathetic and licentious simpletons at heart, and therefore have no one else to blame for their plight but themselves.

In accordance with this position, these same people are of the curious opinion that the Philippines has too much democracy, that it requires a more iron hand that will reign in the unruly currents and vagaries that are inherent in a liberal democracy. The basic formula works like this: less democracy-plus-more discipline can only be beneficial.

First, to address the discipline issue: there is a tendency among the proponents of this argument to compare the "permissive" character of Philippine society, politics, and economics to Singapore's controlled socio-political system, considered by many to be an ideal model of governance. It was former Singaporean premier Lee Kuan Yew who once referred to the

Philippines as a "soft, forgiving culture." In other words, a country wanting indiscipline.

In a 1992 speech in Manila, Lee stated that "I believe that what a country needs to develop is discipline more than democracy. The exuberance of democracy leads to undisciplined and disorderly conditions." The speech's message could not have been lost on Filipino policymakers. Lee received both plaudits and criticisms from Filipinos for expressing what seemed to some to be the obvious, but to others an example of an arrogant guest telling his hosts how to run their household.

Lee's recommendation was yet another simplistic solution to a complicated problem. Unfortunately, in my various discussions with Filipinos and FilAms about the Philippines, I have found that there is a good deal of concurrence among them concerning the need for greater discipline in the home country.

Two things in response: Lee Kuan Yew presided over Singapore, a vastly smaller territory with a vastly smaller population than the Philippines. So just on size and scale alone his counsel is terribly out of whack with reality and a figment of his authoritarian imagination. In short, it's a case of apples and oranges—what might have worked for Lee's tiny island nation will not work for the Philippines.

The other thing is how can you impose discipline on a populace that is in the throes of chronic economic hardship and poverty? As my old professor once said, if you try to tell a starving person in Somalia that what they need most is discipline, that person is likely to kick your rear end. For a person mired in an environment of destitution on one end and hopelessness on the other, indeed an environment not of their own making, the notion of discipline is meaningless in the face of everyday survival. This would be self-evident to any respectable Filipino or FilAm if not for the near- pathological ignorance so many of them display in understanding the Philippines and its people and what they are going through.

Now to the question of democracy. A past has been contrived in which the trappings of liberal democracy in the Philippines were intended to pass for a genuinely substantiative democratic system. But there has never been a full-fledged democracy in the Philippines, not with a socio-economic and political structure that has historically ensured that the rich and powerful retain dominance over the masses. The economic and political elite in the Philippines have been selling a fraudulent bill of democratic goods to the public for decades. Their hegemony is a monument to the perpetual crisis of democracy in the Philippines, a crisis that has monopolistic self-interest, as well as the distinction that separates a meritocracy from a plutocracy.

Real democracy is a system that is transparent, egalitarian, popularly representative, a system where the rule of law holds sway and where, according to Aristotle, "the multitude must of necessity be sovereign and the decision of the majority must be final...so that it results that in democracies the poor are more powerful than the rich."

As Philippine columnist Conrado De Quiros wrote recently, "Each time I hear a public figure proposing a shift to some kind of authoritarian rule because democracy is weak or inapplicable to countries like ours, I don't know whether to laugh or cry. The notion presupposes that we've tried democracy and failed. In fact, the question is: What democracy?"

Ooooo

26
Why I Publish/Reprint Books

Tatay Jobo Elizes
Self-Publisher

Writings are timeless and they act as mirrors to history. I publish writings as they remain relevant anytime. I have seen a lot of good writings in the internet, in magazines and newspapers. But most writers have only one or two articles and therefore not enough material to be published as a book. And yet, many of them need to be published or archived. There are also writers who write a lot but never publish them. There are also old books with no more prints available. The solution is to publish/reprint. I do this for free because of the print-books-on-demand (POD) system, but the printed or hardcopy is not free The printed book will always be there among your collections or libraries. Not all use the internet. The internet access has its technical problems. I can produce fiction, non-fiction, in color also.

My booklist can be seen at
http://tinyurl.com/mj76ccq (copy and paste)
Permission had been granted by the author/ authors to print their books under my free self-publishing service. They own copyrights to their works. Interested reader may request free reading of any of my books, articles or essays via online reading or ebook. Just email me.

Thank you

ooooo